KENNETH LO'S
Chinese
COOKERY COURSE

KENNETH LO'S

Chinese

COOKERY COURSE

THAMES MACDONALD

Editorial Manager
Robin Cross

Art Director
Richard Johnson

Designer
Janet James

Production John Moulder
Illustrations Lucy Su
Jacket photography Chris King

Originally published to
accompany Thames Television's
'A Taste of China'

Produced and directed by
Edward Joffe

Associate Producer
Frederica Lord

First published 1982
Reprinted 1983
Macdonald & Co (Publishers) Ltd
Maxwell House
74 Worship Street
London EC2A 2EN

Printed by Waterlow Ltd., Dunstable

ISBN 0 356 06162 7

CONTENTS

INTRODUCTION

Chinese cooking is noted not only for its wide variety of ingredients and seasonings, but also for the range of cooking methods employed. And within these methods a great refinement in the use of heat has developed, particularly in the use of multi-phase heat for cooking. Thus there are various kinds of stir-frying and quick stir-frying according to the degree of heat used: quick open steaming and slow closed steaming; quick boiling, with periods of slow cooking in the decreasing heat, and long slow clear simmering. There is braising, roasting, deep frying, shallow frying and paper wrapped deep frying. Add that one meal might involve using several of these techniques and one can understand why most Westerners have the impression that Chinese cooking is extremely complicated.

In fact, once you have grasped the basic principles, there is a great deal of flexibility in Chinese cooking, which enables the cook to use whatever materials he or she has on hand. Because of the wide range of dishes which can be prepared with different flavouring and cooking methods, the cook has a wide range of options. Any Westerner cooking Chinese for the first time is usually appalled at the prospect of having to produce half a dozen different dishes which must all be ready at the same time, especially when they involve a variety of cooking techniques – some of them quite complex. The purpose of this course is to give the reader some guidance in this situation.

HOW THE BOOK IS ORGANISED

Each chapter in the book is organised into a meal comprising 5 or 6 dishes, with various options and alternatives. Each chapter also features one main ingredient – rice, noodles, meat, poultry, fish, seafood, vegetables – which the rest of the dishes are built around, to make a complete meal. These dishes are selected to complement one another, not only in the use of ingredients but in the cooking techniques involved. Some have also been selected because they illustrate methods which are significantly different from Western cooking.

The meals may be larger than a novice would want to try when cooking Chinese for the first time, but you are free to prune the menu down by 2 or 3 dishes and still retain the essential feature – the contrasting dishes – of a well-balanced meal. Trying these menus will also be a valuable lesson in how a Chinese meal is put together. Choosing the right dishes is not only an integral part of learning how to cook a Chinese meal, it also provides valuable knowledge if you want to eat well when visiting a Chinese restaurant.

One of the guiding principles in Chinese cooking is to produce freshly cooked, fresh-tasting dishes. Freshness in fact is the keynote, and this is probably one of the reasons why Chinese cooking is said to be healthy. Another reason is that the rich succulent dishes are usually consumed with plain bulk food, such as plain boiled rice or noodles, and washed down with light, clear soup and plenty of fresh vegetables, so that no meal need be too rich.

When planning a meal it is important to remember that all the many cooking techniques fall into two categories. Basically, the Chinese cook their food quickly, at high heat, or they cook it slowly at low heat. The many traditional methods are all variations of these two basic principles.

Tender fresh meat and vegetables are usually cooked in a matter of minutes or even seconds by the stir-frying method in order to retain their natural flavour and juiciness. On the other hand, the tougher ingredients, especially the cheaper cuts of meat, are given a long slow cooking to extract all the goodness from the food and produce dishes of great richness and succulence. These dishes produce wonderful gravies and sauces which go perfectly with plain, boiled rice.

In composing the dishes for a Chinese meal or menu, it is essential to start with one or two long-cooked dishes (stewed, simmered or long-braised) which can be relegated to the back of the cooker or into the oven or steamer to cook on their own, and in their own good time, so as to make room and time for the quick-cooked dishes (stir-fried, deep fried, quick-roast or quick-steamed) each of which may require only a few minutes to prepare. Although there is a misconception that all Chinese dishes require hours to prepare, the truth is that the vast majority of them seldom require more than 10–20 minutes to prepare and cook. These usually fall into the categories of braised, sautéd dishes, or dishes like soup, noodles and rice which can be cooked first, set aside and given a last-minute heat up at the end.

In preparing a sizeable Chinese meal of more than 5 or 6 dishes, it is important to divide the dishes into their respective categories: the long-cooked, the medium-length-cooked and the quick-cooked dishes. Once you have slotted them into their appropriate categories, you will find that there is plenty of time to attend to them all, without any panic.

RICE

PLAIN BOILED RICE
VEGETABLE RICE
SIMPLE FRIED RICE
WATERCRESS AND EGG FLOWER SOUP
STEAMED WHOLE FISH
STIR-FRIED EGGS WITH SHRIMPS
SWEET AND SOUR SPARE RIBS
QUICK-FRIED BEAN SPROUTS WITH GARLIC
AND SPRING ONION
HAINAN CHICKEN RICE

We start with rice – partly because rice is the staple food of China and is served with almost every meal (except at banquets), and partly because without the bulk and blandness of rice the succession of savoury dishes served at a Chinese meal would be too rich to consume in quantity. Indeed, a good many dishes, with richly flavoured gravies, are almost designed specifically to be eaten with rice.

The cooking of rice has become the subject of great controversy in the West. In China, the preparation and cooking of rice is something that is taken for granted. But in the West the cooking of rice has acquired great mystique, with complicated procedures for washing, boiling, straining, drying etc, so that people think of it as something difficult.

We start off with the simplest way of all – the way the Chinese normally eat it at lunch or dinner. We then go on to the three other main ways of dealing with rice – fried rice, vegetable rice and chicken rice, the latter being an easy way of cooking a self-contained meal. These dishes are complemented by four or five savoury dishes and a soup, which the Chinese find useful for washing down rice and other foods during a meal (especially as water is not drunk during meals). The savoury dishes consist of at least one long-cooked dish, in addition to a braised or sautéd one, followed by two quick stir-fried dishes.

Of course, the reader is not obliged to prepare all the dishes in the chapter for a single meal. You simply need to cook one of the rice dishes given, together with two or three savoury dishes (one of which should be long-cooked), plus a soup. Similarly, the number of dishes can be increased if you are preparing a meal for more than half-a-dozen people.

PLAIN BOILED RICE

Serves 4–6

1lb (450g) long-grain rice
approximately 1¼ times equivalent volume
of cold water: about 18 fl.oz (500ml)

Rinse the rice twice under cold running water, then drain. Place the rice and water in a saucepan with a tight-fitting lid. Bring to the boil, then reduce heat to very low, simmer gently for 8–10 minutes. Turn off the heat (but do not take off the lid) and let the rice stand and cook in its own heat for another 10 minutes.

At the end of this time the rice should have absorbed all the water and become dry and flaky.

VEGETABLE RICE

Serves 4–6

1lb (450g) long-grain rice
approximately 18 fl.oz (500ml) cold water
2½ tablespoons vegetable oil
1½ tablespoons lard or butter
8oz (225g) spring greens or spring cabbage
4oz (100g) peas
1½ teaspoons salt
1–2 tablespoons soy sauce (optional)

Repeat the instructions for plain boiled rice, up to the point where the rice comes to the boil. Boil for 2 minutes then turn off the heat. Leave the lid of the saucepan on.

Heat the vegetable oil and lard in a saucepan. Cut the spring greens into 1 inch (2.5cm) slices and place in the saucepan with the peas. Sprinkle evenly with salt and stir-fry over moderate heat for 1 minute.

Pour the partially cooked rice on top of the vegetables and pack down with a wooden spoon. Turn the heat to low and simmer gently for 8 minutes with the lid on. Turn the heat off and let the rice stand and cook in its own heat for a further 8 minutes.

Turn out on to a large serving dish so that the green vegetables are on top of the rice. Some soy sauce may be poured on top of the vegetables before serving.

SIMPLE FRIED RICE

Fried rice is ideal to serve with almost all Chinese savoury dishes, meat, poultry, fish, seafood or vegetables.

Serves 4–5

4 tablespoons vegetable oil
2 medium-sized onions, sliced
3 rashers bacon, cut into strips
4 tablespoons peas, fresh or frozen
2 eggs lightly beaten
2 tablespoons light soy sauce

Heat oil in a large frying pan. When it is hot add the onion and bacon and stir-fry for two minutes. Add the peas and shrimps and stir with the onions and bacon for $1\frac{1}{2}$ minutes. Push the mixture to one side and tilt the pan so that the oil collects on the other side. Pour the beaten eggs into the oil. When it has slightly set scramble the egg with a fork. Add the rice to the pan and mix well with the other ingredients. Continue mixing for approximately 2 minutes until the rice is heated through.

Sprinkle the fried rice with soy sauce and serve in a large, well-heated serving bowl.

WATERCRESS AND EGG FLOWER SOUP

These light soups are intended to be consumed, a mouthful or so at a time, throughout the meal – in place of water.

Serves 4–5

2 pints (1.15 l) stock
1 chicken stock cube
$1\frac{1}{2}$ teaspoons salt
pepper to taste
2 eggs, lightly beaten
1 bundle watercress, chopped
2 stalks spring onion, cut into $\frac{1}{4}$ inch shreds
1 teaspoon sesame oil (optional)

Heat the stock in a saucepan and add the stock cube, salt and pepper, bring to the boil then reduce heat to a simmer. Pour the beaten egg into the soup in a thin stream along the prongs of a fork, letting it trail over the whole surface of the soup. When the egg has set (in about 3–4 minutes), add the watercress. Bring back to the boil, and sprinkle the top of the soup with the spring onions. Turn the heat off, adjust the seasoning and sprinkle with sesame oil.

Serve in individual soup bowls or in a large soup tureen.

STEAMED WHOLE FISH

This is probably the most popular way of cooking fish in China. It is ideal for small whole fish, such as trout or mullet, and even for fillets of larger fish.

Serves 4–5

fish (trout, mullet, carp, sea-bass etc)
2 teaspoons salt
pepper to taste
6 slices root ginger, shredded
4 spring onion stalks, shredded
6 tablespoons vegetable oil
2 tablespoons soy sauce
2 tablespoons dry sherry

Rub the fish inside and out with salt, pepper and a half tablespoon of oil. Put a quarter of the shredded ginger and spring onion inside the fish and sprinkle another quarter on top. Place the fish on an oval heat-proof dish, lay it in a steamer and steam over vigorously boiling water for 15–18 minutes. Remove the dish from the steamer, discard the ginger and spring onion and pour away liquid that has accumulated in the dish. Pour the soy sauce and sherry over the fish, and arrange the remaining shredded ginger and spring onion on the top.

Heat the vegetable oil in a small pan until it is smoking hot. Pour the hot oil in a thin stream over the full length of the fish. This helps to impregnate the fish with the flavours of the freshness of the onion and ginger which, together with the flavour of the sherry and the soy sauce, seem to add to the quality of the dish.

The fish is served whole. Guests help themselves, dipping each portion in the sauce before transferring it to their rice bowl. This dish should be served with rice and some other savoury dishes.

STIR-FRIED EGGS WITH SHRIMPS

This is a simple but satisfying dish which can be prepared quickly, to be served with rice.

Serves 4–5

4–5 eggs
2 teaspoons salt
4oz (100g) shrimps (fresh or frozen)
½ teaspoon freshly ground pepper
3 spring onion stalks, cut into ¼ inch (5mm) shreds
5 tablespoons vegetable oil
2 tablespoons dry sherry
2 tablespoons soy sauce

Beat the eggs lightly with 1 teaspoon of salt. Season the shrimps with the remaining salt and half the pepper. Heat the oil in a frying pan. Add the shrimps and the spring onions. Stir-fry quickly over medium heat for 1½ minutes, then push to one side. Pour in the egg and when it is about to set – in about 1½ minutes – stir in the egg mixture. Stir-fry for 2–3 minutes, then sprinkle with the remainder of the spring onion, pepper and sherry.

Turn out on to a well-heated serving dish and sprinkle with soy sauce.

SWEET AND SOUR SPARE-RIBS

Spare ribs can be served on their own, as a starter or snack, or in the context of the meal in conjunction with rice. On their own, they are best served crisp and dry, but when they are served as part of a meal they are best served with sauce, and should be cooked slightly longer in order to make the meat more easily detachable from the bone. This dish of sweet and sour spare-ribs is meant to be eaten with rice.

Serves 4–5

3lb (1.5kg) spare-ribs
1½ teaspoons salt
pepper (to taste)
4 tablespoons vegetable oil
½ tablespoon star anise (optional)
4 tablespoons vegetable oil
3 tablespoons soy sauce
2 tablespoons hoisin sauce (optional)
¼ pint (200ml) stock

SAUCE:
1 tablespoon vegetable oil
1 medium green pepper, cut into strips
1 medium-sized onion, thinly sliced
3 tablespoons sugar
5 tablespoons wine vinegar
2 tablespoons tomato puree
4 tablespoons orange juice
4 tablespoons water or stock
2 tablespoons cornflour, blended in 7–8 tablespoons water
2½ tablespoons vegetable oil

Preheat the oven to 200°C (400°F, gas mark 6).

Season the spare-ribs with the salt and pepper, and rub with 1 tablespoon of oil.

Heat the remaining oil in a casserole. Add the spare-ribs and turn them in the hot oil for 2–3 minutes over the high heat. Add all the other ingredients, including the stock. Turn the ribs in the stock until it starts to boil, then reduce the heat to low and simmer gently for a few minutes.

Put the casserole into the preheated oven for 25 minutes then reduce the heat to 160°C (325°F, gas mark 3) for 30–35 minutes. Meanwhile make the sauce. Heat the oil in a frying pan and stir-fry the pepper and onion for 2–3 minutes. Add all the other ingredients and stir quickly until the mixture is well blended and the sauce has thickened and become translucent.

Remove the casserole from the oven. Stir the spare-ribs gently, then pour in the sauce. Place the casserole over low heat and stir until the sauce is evenly blended with the spare-ribs. Serve in the casserole or turn out onto a large heated serving dish.

QUICK-FRIED BEAN SPROUTS WITH GARLIC AND SPRING ONION

Serves 4–6

4 tablespoons vegetable oil
3 slices root ginger, shredded
2 teaspoons salt
1oz (25g) Szechuan Ja Chai pickles (optional), shredded
3 cloves garlic, crushed
1lb (450g) bean sprouts, washed and drained
1 tablespoon lard
2 tablespoons soy sauce
1 tablespoon vinegar
2 tablespoons stock
2 teaspoons sesame oil
3 spring onion stalks, cut into ½ inch (1cm) strips

Heat the oil in a saucepan or large frying pan. Add the ginger, salt, pickles and garlic. Stir over medium heat for 1 minute. Turn the heat to high and add the bean sprouts. Stir-fry for 2 minutes, then add the lard, soy sauce, vinegar and stock. Continue to stir-fry for 1 minute then sprinkle with sesame oil and spring onions. Stir-fry for a further half-minute then serve immediately.

HAINAN CHICKEN RICE

Hainan island is the southernmost province of China. Its chicken rice is easy to produce, yet satisfying. It is included here because it is a dish which can be produced and eaten independently of other dishes, as a meal on its own.

Serves 5–6

3–3½lb (1.3–1.5kg) chicken
1lb (400g) rice
2 cloves garlic
3 slices root ginger
1 tablespoon salt
2 chicken stock cubes
8–12oz (225–350g) leeks, cut into 1½ inch
   (3.5cm) lengths
4oz (100g) peas

DIP SAUCE:
2 tablespoons vinegar
5 tablespoons soy sauce
2 cloves garlic, crushed
1 tablespoon sesame oil

Using a heavy meat chopper or a heavy knife and a mallet, chop the chicken through the bone into 18–20 bite-size pieces. Place the rice in a saucepan in half its own volume of water and cover tightly. Bring to the boil and boil for two minutes. Turn off the heat and leave to stand to absorb all the water. Give each clove of garlic a blow with the side of the chopper.

Put the chicken pieces in a casserole with 2½ pints (1.4 l) water and bring to the boil. Skim for impurities after 5 minutes. Add the ginger and salt, reduce the heat to low and simmer gently for 45 minutes.

Remove the chicken pieces with a slotted spoon and reserve. Put the stock cubes, leeks, garlic and peas into the casserole and bring to the boil. Pour the rice into the casserole and mix well. Simmer gently for 10 minutes or until the rice has absorbed all the stock. Arrange the chicken pieces on top of the rice, put on the lid and turn off the heat.

To make the dip sauce, mix together the vinegar, soy sauce, crushed garlic and sesame oil.

To serve, bring the casserole to the table, and divide the dip sauce into 2 small dishes. The guests help themselves to the rice and vegetables, dipping each piece of chicken into the sauce before eating.

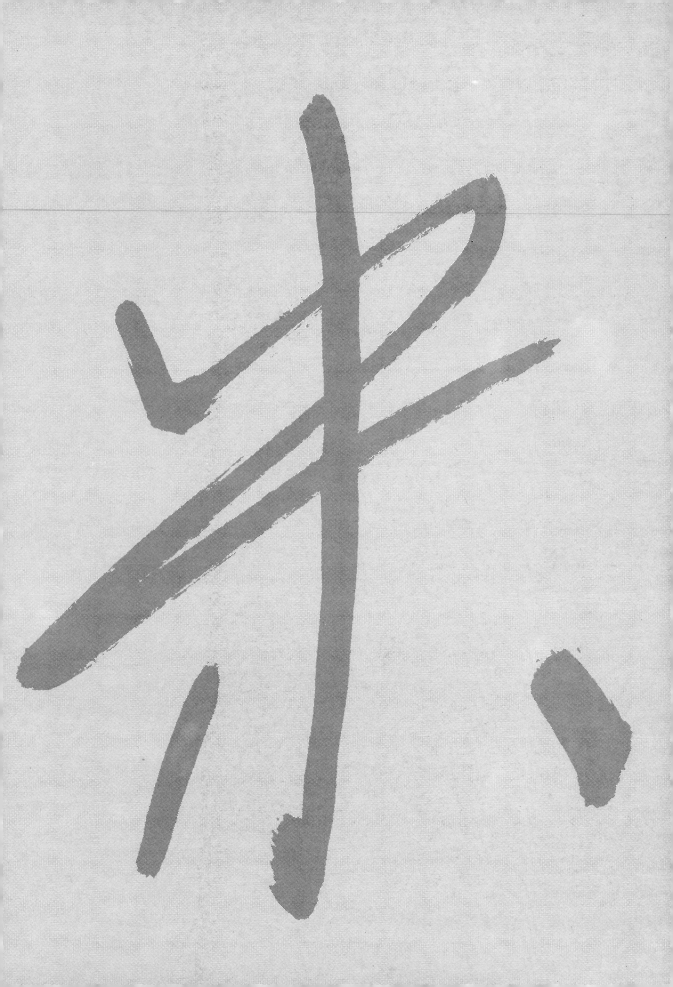

NOODLES

SIMPLE CHOW MEIN OR STIR-FRIED NOODLES
NOODLES WITH LONG-BRAISED SOY BEEF
WITH BROCCOLI
QUICK-FRIED SHREDDED LAMB WITH SPRING ONIONS
QUICK-FRIED MIXED 'THREE SEA FLAVOURS'
IN BLACK BEAN SAUCE
QUICK-FRIED AND QUICK-BRAISED GINGER
AND ONION CRABS
PEKING JA CHIANG MEIN NOODLES
SOUP OF THE THREE SHREDDED INGREDIENTS

It is not certain who first started to make noodles, the Chinese or the Italians, but certainly noodles have been eaten in China for more than 2000 years. Among the 26 documented millionaires of the early Han Dynasty (about 500–400BC) were a number who made their money from flour and noodles.

There are three main types of noodles eaten in China today. Wheat flour noodles are the most widely used, and are consumed in quantities in the North, where wheats are grown. They are often tossed with meat sauces and served as a whole meal. Rice flour noodles are most popular in South China, where rice is grown in abundance. Because of the long South-East coastline, seafood is plentiful and is often found served with noodles – sometimes just as a snack. Pea starch noodles (also called transparent noodles) are whiteish and semi-opaque. They are often added to soups, gravies and to mixed meat and vegetable dishes to provide extra texture and variety.

SIMPLE CHOW MEIN OR STIR-FRIED NOODLES

Chow Mein is the best known noodle dish. It differs from the Italian spaghettis in that the noodles are first boiled then fried in oil and flavourings before being topped with meat and vegetables.

Serves 3–4

1lb (450g) Chinese noodles (or spaghetti)
2 tablespoons dried shrimps
1 medium-sized onion, thinly sliced
6oz (150g) pork, or 4 rashers bacon, cut into shreds
3oz (75g) French beans or snow peas
1½ teaspoons salt
4 tablespoons vegetable oil
½ chicken stock cube, dissolved in 5 tablespoons hot stock or water
6oz (150g) bean sprouts
2 tablespoons soy sauce
1 tablespoon lard or butter
3 spring onion stalks, cut into 1 inch (2.5cm) lengths
2 tablespoons dry sherry

Boil the noodles for 5–6 minutes (or spaghetti for 17–18 minutes) then drain and rinse under running water. Soak dried shrimps for 20–25 minutes and drain.

Heat the oil in a large frying pan. Add the onion, shrimps, pork and french beans. Stir-fry together for 2½ minutes. Add the stock and stir-fry for another 1½ minutes. Remove half the mixture and reserve. Add the bean sprouts and noodles, sprinkle on 1 tablespoon soy sauce and stir with the other ingredients until well mixed and thoroughly heated through (about 2½ minutes). Turn the mixture out on to a large, heated serving dish.

Meanwhile, add the lard to the frying pan. When it has melted, return the reserved mixture to the pan, together with the spring onions, 1 tablespoon soy sauce and 2 tablespoons sherry. Turn the heat to high. When the mixture begins to bubble, turn and stir a few times, then pour on top of the noodles in the serving dish.

Chow Mein can be made more elaborate simply by adding a few more ingredients. Mushrooms, preferably Chinese dried mushrooms, soaked for 20 minutes in water and shredded, during the first stage of the stir-frying. Fresh shrimps or prawns are added at the following stage, when the stock is added. You need only add 4–5 medium sized mushrooms and 3–4oz (75–100g) fresh shrimps or prawns, but they will add a good deal of interest and flavour to the dish.

In Chinese cooking all subsidiary foods are cut to the same shape as the principal ingredient. In the case of noodles they are all cut into the shape of noodles, ie into match-stick strips. The various vegetables are meant to contribute to the freshness of the dish, whilst the meats and dried ingredients which are fried together with the onions are meant to contribute to the richness of the dish by impregnating the oil in which they are fried with their flavours.

Another familiar and popular way of serving noodles is to add a half bowlful of long-cooked (usually soy-braised) meat together with its gravy on top of the bowl of plain boiled noodles, garnished with some chopped spring onions and perhaps with lightly cooked vegetables such as flowerets of broccoli or cauliflower or some blanched and stir-fried beans or snow peas.

NOODLES WITH LONG-BRAISED SOY BEEF WITH BROCCOLI

This warming hearty dish is often served as a self-contained meal on its own, rather than as part of a large meal.

Serves 4–5

1lb (450g) Chinese noodles, or spaghetti
8–12oz (225–350g) broccoli or cauliflower, divided into florets
2–3 tablespoons vegetable oil
2–3 slices root ginger
2 small onions, thinly sliced
1¼lb (575g) chuck steak or stewing beef, cut into bite-size pieces
1 teaspoon salt
3 tablespoons soy sauce
2 tablespoons star anise
½ tablespoon sugar
1 pint (600ml) water
1 chicken stock cube
1 tablespoon cornflour, blended with 3 tablespoons water
2 tablespoons dry sherry

Boil the noodles for 5–6 minutes (or spaghetti for 17–18 minutes). Add the broccoli or cauliflower for the last 5 minutes. Drain and rinse under running water.

Preheat oven to 200°C (400°F, gas mark 6).

Heat the oil in a casserole. Add the ginger, onion and beef and sprinkle with salt. Stir-fry over high heat for 3½ minutes, then add soy sauce, anise, sugar and water. Bring to the boil, then put the casserole in the preheated oven for half an hour. Take the casserole out, stir well, reduce heat to 160°C (325°F, gas mark 3) and put back in the oven for 1½ hours. Stir twice during this time.

Take the casserole out of the oven and put it on top of the cooker on low heat. Add the stock cube and the blended cornflour. Stir over low heat until the gravy thickens. Add the sherry and stir again. To serve, pour a kettleful of boiling water over the noodles and vegetables placed in a colander. After draining, divide the noodles and vegetables into 4 or 5 separate bowls and spoon meat and sauce on top. Sprinkle each bowl with some chopped spring onion and serve.

At a full-scale meal noodles, like rice, can be served with any group of savoury dishes: in particular with dishes that have ample sauce or gravy. However, there is one category of dishes which are seldom served with noodles, that is fish dishes. Perhaps because fish with bones would be dangerous, gulped down with a mouthful of noodles, which is how noodles are best eaten and enjoyed.

On the other hand, shredded and stir-fried dishes are particularly suitable with noodles, as they are already cut in the same shape – in thin strips – and are therefore easy to mix together. Seafood is also particularly suitable for serving with noodles partly because it is generally highly savoury, which when it is consumed in the same mouthful with noodles, tends to make the latter equally savoury and appealing.

The 2 stir-fried dishes which follow are highly suitable to serve with noodles; in addition a dish of 'onion and ginger crab' which like the other dishes can be used as a substantial garnish to place on top of a simple Chow Mein or stir-fried noodles.

QUICK-FRIED SHREDDED LAMB WITH SPRING ONION

This dish can be served, along with other savoury dishes, to be eaten with rice or noodles; or it can be poured on top of a large dish of simply cooked noodles or Chow Mein. Noodle enthusiasts often prefer to eat savoury dishes with noodles rather than rice.

Serves 3–4

1¼lb (575g) leg of lamb
1 teaspoon salt
4½ tablespoons vegetable oil
3 cloves garlic, coarsely chopped
1½ tablespoons yellow bean sauce
1½ tablespoons soy sauce
1½ tablespoons hoisin sauce
2 tablespoons stock
2 tablespoons dry sherry
4 spring onion stalks, cut into 2 inch (5cm) sections

Cut the lamb into small thin strips. Sprinkle with salt and half tablespoon of oil.

Heat remaining oil in a wok or large frying pan. Add the lamb and garlic and stir-fry over high heat for 1½ minutes. Add the sauces and stir-fry with the lamb for another 1½ minutes. Add the stock, sherry, and spring onion. Stir quickly for 1 more minute.

QUICK-FRIED MIXED 'THREE SEA FLAVOURS' IN BLACK BEAN SAUCE

Again this can be served as one of several savoury dishes in a meal, or it can be poured on top of a dish of noodles and served as a meal in itself.

Serves 4–5

8oz (225g) large prawns (fresh or frozen)
5oz (150g) scallops
1½ tablespoons cornflour
1 egg white
5oz (150g) squid
3 slices root ginger, finely chopped
3 stalks green celery, cut into 2 inch (5cm) strips
1½ teaspoons salt
4 tablespoons vegetable oil

SAUCE:
2/3 tablespoons black beans, soaked, drained and finely chopped
2 cloves garlic, finely chopped
1–2 chillis, finely chopped
2 spring onion stalks, finely chopped
2 tablespoons oil
5 tablespoons good stock
2 tablespoons dry sherry
1½ tablespoons cornflour blended in 4 tablespoons water

Cut the prawns into 3 slices and the scallops into 2 slices. Dust with cornflour and wet with egg white. Cut the squid into 1½ inch (3.5cm) strips, then cut each strip half way through with half a dozen criss-cross cuts.

Heat the oil in a wok or frying-pan. Add the ginger, prawns, scallops, squid and celery and salt. Stir-fry over high heat for 2½ minutes. Remove with slotted spoon and reserve. Place all the solid ingredients for the sauce in the pan with 2 tablespoons oil. Stir-fry for 1 minute then add stock and sherry and stir-fry over high heat for 2 more minutes. Pour in the blended cornflour and stir until the sauce thickens. Return all the seafood to the pan together with the celery. Stir-fry over high heat for a further 1 minute.

DEEP-FRIED AND QUICK-BRAISED GINGER AND ONION CRABS

To enjoy this dish to the full, suck the delicious sauce from the shell before tackling the crab meat. It can also be served poured over a dish of noodles or Chow Mein.

Serves 4–5

3 medium-sized crabs
1 pint (600ml) oil
6 slices root ginger, shredded
4 spring onion stalks, cut in 2 inch (5cm) pieces
⅓ pint (200ml) chicken stock
2 tablespoons soy sauce
1½ teaspoons salt
3 tablespoons dry sherry
2 tablespoons vinegar
1½ tablespoons cornflour blended in 4 tablespoons water
2 teaspoons sesame oil

Remove the main shell of each crab. Chop the body into 4–5 pieces, each with a leg or claw attached. Crack the claws.

Heat the oil in a deep fryer or 1 pint (600ml) oil in a deep frying pan or wok. When a crumb sizzles when dropped into the oil add the crab, piece by piece. Turn in the oil over high heat for 2½ minutes. Remove the crab with a slotted spoon and pour off the oil. Add the ginger and spring onion and stir-fry for ½ minute. Pour in the stock and soy sauce, and return the crab pieces to the pan, turning them rapidly in the boiling sauce. Sprinkle first with salt, and then with the sherry and vinegar. Continue to stir for 1½ minutes, then place a lid over the pan and close firmly, leaving the contents to cook for 2 minutes.

Open the lid and sprinkle evenly with the blended cornflour. Turn the crab pieces over a few times in the thickened sauce.

Transfer to a heated, deep-sided dish, sprinkle with sesame oil and serve.

PEKING JA CHIANG MEIN NOODLES

Fresh noodles are available in Chinese food stores. Dried noodles, which are more widely available, require a longer cooking time – 10–15 minutes.

1lb (450g) hand-drawn, home-made noodles or spaghetti
3–4 dried mushrooms
4oz (100g) bean sprouts
½ chicken stock cube
5 tablespoons stock
4 tablespoons vegetable oil
2 slices root ginger, finely chopped
2 cloves garlic, finely chopped
1 medium-sized onion, finely chopped
½ teaspoon salt
1lb (450g) minced pork or beef
1½ tablespoons soy sauce
1½ tablespoons yellow bean sauce
1½ tablespoons cornflour blended in 4 tablespoons water
3–4 spring onion stalks, cut into 2 inch strips
1 cucumber cut into matchstick strips

Boil the noodles for 3–4 minutes (or spaghetti for 17–18 minutes), drain and rinse under running water. Soak the dried mushrooms for 20 minutes in hot water. Drain, remove and discard stalk and chop caps finely. Parboil bean sprouts for 1 minute then drain. Crumble and dissolve the stock cube in the stock.

Heat the oil in a wok or large frying pan. Add the ginger, garlic, onion, mushrooms and salt. Stir-fry over high heat for 1½ minutes, then add minced meat and stir-fry together for 3½ minutes. Add soy sauce, yellow bean sauce and stock. Continue to stir-fry for 2½ minutes, then reduce heat and leave to cook for another 2½ minutes. Pour in the blended cornflour and stir until the mixture thickens.

To serve, pour boiling water over the noodles, then drain immediately and thoroughly. Place the noodles in a deep-sided dish. Pour the meat sauce over the centre of the noodles and arrange the bean sprouts, spring onions and shredded cucumber around the sides. At the table, the host tosses all the ingredients together before serving the guest.

SOUP OF THE THREE SHREDDED INGREDIENTS

After a succession of highly flavoured dishes it is customary to serve a light fresh-tasting soup.

Serves 4–5

3–4oz (75–100g) chicken breast meat,
   shredded
½ teaspoon salt
2 teaspoons cornflour
1 egg white
2 pints (1.15 l) chicken stock
1 chicken stock cube
1 medium-sized cucumber, cut into
   matchstick shreds
3oz (75g) ham, shredded
salt and pepper
1 teaspoon sesame oil

Toss the shredded chicken in salt and cornflour, and then in half the egg white. Parboil the shredded chicken in a wire basket in boiling water for ½ minute then drain.

Meanwhile heat the chicken stock in a saucepan. When it starts to boil add the stock-cube, cucumber, chicken and ham. Bring back to the boil, then reduce the heat and simmer for 3 minutes. Add salt and pepper to taste. Sprinkle with sesame oil and serve in a large soup tureen.

鶏
鴨

POULTRY

RED-COOKED CHICKEN
STEAMED CHICKEN IN GROUND RICE
PEKING DUCK
PANCAKES
MU SHU ROU
SPRING ROLLS
QUICK-FRIED RIBBON OF DUCK WITH SHREDDED
GINGER WITH CHILLI AND MUSTARD SAUCE
QUICK-FRIED DICED CHICKEN CUBES WITH
WALNUTS IN SOY PASTE SAUCE
SLICED CHICKEN AND MUSHROOM SOUP
WITH LETTUCE

Chicken and duck are seldom mass-produced in China, so it is always an occasion when one of these birds appears on the table. A bird, in fact, tends to be produced whenever an extra dish is required for an extra treat. The appearance of a dish of chicken on the table in China always brings a sense of occasion.

Duck is something more special, and Peking Duck is only obtainable in specialist restaurants. Duck are plentiful only near duck farms, lakes or waterways, especially along the Yangtze river, whereas there are chickens everywhere, reared on every peasant smallholding or backyard.

There are numerous ways of cooking duck or chicken, and literally hundreds of dishes which can be prepared with them.

One of the more common ways of cooking chicken is in soy sauce, often called red-cooked. Chinese stews of meat or poultry differ from Western stews mainly in the addition of root ginger, sugar and soy sauce. Ginger helps to take away any unwanted taste in the bird; soy sauce enhances the flavour and sugar helps to enrich it.

RED-COOKED CHICKEN

Serves 6–8

1 chicken about 3½–4½lb (1.5–2kg)
5 slices root ginger
6–7 tablespoons soy sauce
1 tablespoon sugar
2–3 spring onion stalks, cut into 1 inch
  (2.5cm) lengths
4–5 tablespoons dry sherry

Dip the chicken in boiling water to parboil for 5 minutes. Remove and drain. Preheat the oven to 190°C (375°F, gas mark 5).

Place the chicken in a casserole. Add soy sauce, ginger, sugar, and ½ pint (300ml) of water. Bring the contents to the boil on top of the cooker, turning the chicken over a few times in the sauce. Close the lid and put the casserole into the oven for 1¼ hours, turning the chicken 3–4 times. Sprinkle the chicken with sherry and spring onion and then return the casserole to the oven to cook for a further 15 minutes.

The chicken can be served by bringing the casserole to the table. The chicken should be sufficiently tender to take to pieces with a pair of chopsticks. The sauce in the casserole is delicious and chicken pieces should be dipped in it before eating. Some of the sauce can also be spooned into the rice in each guest's rice bowl.

STEAMED CHICKEN IN GROUND RICE

Ground rice is often used in China in much the same way as bread crumbs are used in the West. The ground rice is often stir-fried in a dry pan until it is brown and aromatic.

Serves 6–8

1 chicken about 3–4lb (1.3–1.75kg)
3 teaspoons salt
1 beaten egg white
5–6oz (150–175g) ground rice
pepper to taste
lettuce or cabbage leaves

DIP SAUCE: (1)
1 tablespoon chicken fat
2 tablespoons chicken stock
1 teaspoon salt
2 tablespoons light soy sauce
3 teaspoons chilli sauce

DIP SAUCE: (2)
1 tablespoon vegetable oil
1½ teaspoons sesame oil
3 teaspoons mustard powder
2 tablespoons chicken stock
1½ teaspoons salt
2 tablespoons soy sauce

Using a meat chopper or heavy knife and mallet, chop the chicken through the bones into 18–20 pieces. Rub with salt and pepper to taste. Leave to season for half an hour. Fry the ground rice in a pan, stirring all the time, until it turns distinctly brownish-yellow and aromatic. Wet the chicken pieces with egg white, and roll them in the ground rice until coated.

Arrange the chicken pieces in a single layer at the bottom of the basket-steamer lined with lettuce or cabbage leaves. Turn the heat high and steam the chicken steadily for 2¼ hours.

Top up the boiling water under the steamer every now and then.

Place the dip ingredients in 2 separate bowls, stirring until amalgamated.

Bring the steam-basket to the dining table, and place the 2 dip-sauce dishes beside the basket for the diners to dip the chicken pieces in. The chicken meat should be tender enough to come away from the bone easily.

PEKING DUCK

Peking Duck is the most famous of all the duck dishes in China. It is in fact a straightforward roast duck. Although there are numerous methods of preparation – some very complicated – the following is probably the simplest and most effective way of cooking it.

1 duck about 3–4lb (1.5–1.75kg)

SAUCE:
2½–3 tablespoons vegetable oil
1 can 6–8oz (175–225g) yellow bean sauce
4–5 tablespoons sugar
2 teaspoons sesame oil

GARNISH:
5–6 spring onion stalks, cut in 2 inch (5cm)
  lengths
1 medium-sized cucumber, cut into
  matchstick shreds

Clean the duck and dry thoroughly by hanging it up to dry in an airy spot for at least 4–5 hours, if possible overnight. If in a hurry, use a hair-drier on it.

Preheat the oven to 200°C (400°F, gas mark 6).

Prepare the sauce by heating the oil in a small heavy saucepan. Add the yellow bean sauce and stir and heat gently over the low heat for 2 minutes. Add the sugar and continue to stir for another 2½–3 minutes.

Add the sesame oil and stir once more.

Place the prepared duck on a wire rack set on top of a roasting pan. Roast for 1¼ hours. The duck requires no basting, and do not open the oven until the duck is ready.

Peking Duck is served by first cutting off the crispy skin in 2 × 1 inch (5 × 2.5cm) slices. The meat is then carved in similar-sized slices. Serve on separate dishes.

To eat, you roll up a piece of skin and meat inside a pancake with a pinch each of cucumber and spring onion. This mouthful is then brushed heavily with the sauce. Before lifting to the mouth, the bottom end of the pancake roll should be turned up so that nothing drops out.

QUICK-FRIED RIBBON OF DUCK WITH SHREDDED GINGER WITH CHILLI AND MUSTARD SAUCE

Serves 4

4 tablespoons vegetable oil
6 slices root ginger, shredded
2 stalks young leeks, shredded
2 sticks celery, shredded
2 teaspoons salt
10oz (275g) duck meat, cut into matchstick
  shreds
1 small red sweet pepper, deseeded and
  shredded
1½ tablespoons lard
2–3 cloves garlic, finely chopped
2 dried chilli peppers, finely chopped
3 teaspoons mustard powder
2 tablespoons light soy sauce
3 tablespoons good stock
1 tablespoon wine vinegar
1–2 teaspoons chilli sauce
2 teaspoons sugar

Heat the oil in a large frying pan. Add the ginger, leeks and celery and stir-fry them over high heat for 2½ minutes. Sprinkle with salt, add duck meat and pepper and continue to stir-fry for 2½ minutes. Remove with slotted spoon and reserve.

Add the lard, garlic, dried chillis, peppers, mustard and stir-fry over high heat for ¾ minute. Add soy sauce, stock, vinegar, chilli sauce and sugar and stir fry all the ingredients together for 1 minute. Return the duck, ginger, leeks and celery to the pan to mix and turn together with the sauce. Turn and stir-fry over the high heat for 1 minute.

This dish should be served on a heated dish and eaten in conjunction with any of the pancake dishes, or with boiled rice along with Red Cooked Chicken.

PANCAKES

1lb (450g) plain flour
1½ teaspoons sugar
1 cup warm water
1 teaspoon vegetable oil
sesame oil for brushing

Sift the flour into a mixing bowl. Stir in the sugar, oil and water. Stir until well-mixed. Knead the mixture into a firm dough and then into two long sausage rolls. Cut each roll into a dozen pieces and form each piece into a small ball. Pat each ball into a round disc. Brush the top of one disc with sesame oil and place a second disc on top to form a 'sandwich'. Use a rolling pin to roll the sandwiches into a pancake about 5–6 inches (13–15cm) in diameter.

Heat a dry frying-pan over low to medium heat. When the pan is hot place a pancake in the pan and shake so that the pancake slides around on the surface of the pan. After about 1½ minutes turn the pancake over with a fish slice and cook in the same way until the pancake begins to puff and some brown spots appear here and there. Now lift the pancake and very gently peel the sandwich apart into its two constituent pancakes. Fold each pancake in half and stack them on a plate. If they are not used immediately they should be covered with a damp cloth. They can be heated up readily by inserting them in a steamer for a few minutes.

These pancakes can be used not just for the Peking Duck but also for other dishes such as the following where pancakes are an integral part of the dish.

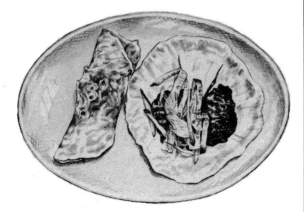

MU SHU ROU

1 dozen Golden Needles or dried tiger lily
    stems
8oz (225g) minced pork
3–4 tablespoons dried 'wood ear' fungi
1 teaspoon salt
5–6 eggs
6 tablespoons vegetable oil
1½ tablespoons soy sauce
1 teaspoon sugar
4oz (100g) bamboo shoots, shredded
1 tablespoon lard
4–5 tablespoons chicken stock
2 tablespoons dry sherry
3–4 spring onion stalks, cut into 2 inch
    (2.5cm) lengths

Clean and soak the tiger lily stems and wood ears in water for 10 minutes, and drain. Add salt to eggs and beat lightly with a fork for 15 seconds.

Heat a wok or frying-pan. Add 2½ tablespoons oil and when the oil is hot then add pork and stir-fry quickly for 2 minutes. Add the soy sauce, sugar, tiger lily stems, 'wood ears' and bamboo shoots.

Stir-fry together quickly for 3 minutes. Remove and put aside. Add the remaining oil and lard to the pan. Tilt until the oil and fat covers the whole surface of the pan. Pour the beaten egg into the middle of the pan. After 1 minute stir and scramble the eggs lightly, then remove the pan from the heat. When the eggs are nearly all set give them one more stir and scramble.

Now return the pork and vegetable mixture to the pan and place it over high heat. Stir and mix the pork and vegetables with the egg, breaking the egg up into ½ inch (1cm) pieces. Add the stock. Stir and turn for 1 minute and sprinkle the contents with the sherry and spring onions. Stir and turn for another half minute. Serve hot.

The Mu Shu Rou is eaten by rolling it (about 2 tablespoons at a time) inside a pancake. The filling is rolled up in the pancake like a sausage roll, and folded up at one end, so that nothing will fall or drip out. Each guest helps himself and rolls up his own pancake.

SPRING ROLLS

Serves 5–6 (about 1 dozen pancakes)

The original spring rolls were probably not the crispy pancake rolls now frequently served in Chinese restaurants abroad. The original ones were probably served to celebrate the spring festival, when pancakes (the same as those used in wrapping 'Peking Duck') were used to roll assortments of shredded quick-fry vegetables, served on separate dishes. The following are three selections of pancake stuffings which should be quick stir-fried separately.

STUFFING 1:
3½ tablespoons vegetable oil
3 cloves garlic, crushed and chopped finely
2 teaspoons salt
2–3 leaves Chinese cabbage or lettuce, shredded
¾–1lb (350–450g) fresh bean sprouts
4 spring onion stalks, cut into 2 inch (5cm) lengths
2 teaspoons sugar
1½ tablespoons soy sauce
1 tablespoon lard

Heat oil in a large frying pan or saucepan. When hot, add the garlic and salt. Stir-fry over high heat for half a minute. Add the lettuce (or Chinese cabbage), spring onion and bean sprouts. Continue to turn and stir-fry over a high heat for 1½ minutes. Serve in a heated dish.

STUFFING 2:
3–4 stalks green celery, shredded
2–3 stalks young leeks, shredded
2–3 fresh young carrots, shredded
2 teaspoons salt
4 large mushrooms
3½ tablespoons vegetable oil
3–4 tablespoons stock
2 tablespoons soy sauce
2 tablespoons hoisin sauce
1 tablespoon lard

Sprinkle the celery, leeks and carrots with salt. Discard stem of mushrooms and shred cap.

Heat the oil in a large frying pan or wok. When hot add the leeks and shredded carrots. Stir-fry over high heat for 2½ minutes. Add the stock and mushrooms and continue to stir until the liquid in the pan is almost dry. Now add the celery, soy sauce, hoisin sauce and lard. Stir-fry for a further 1½ minutes and serve on a heated dish.

STUFFING 3:
3½ tablespoons vegetable oil
4–5oz (100–150g) snow peas or mange tout, shredded
3–4oz (75–100g) bamboo shoots, shredded
2–3oz (75–100g) French beans, shredded
1 red pepper, shredded
1–2 chilli peppers, deseeded and shredded
1 teaspoon salt
3 tablespoons stock
2 tablespoons soy sauce
2 teaspoons chilli sauce
1 tablespoon vinegar
1 tablespoon lard
2 teaspoons sesame oil

Heat the oil in a large frying-pan or wok. When hot, add all the vegetables together with the salt. Stir-fry quickly over high heat for 2 minutes. Add the stock, soy sauce, chilli sauce and vinegar. Continue to stir-fry for 1½ minutes. Add the lard and sesame oil, stir a few more times and serve.

Serve the three dishes together. They should provide ample choice for guests stuffing their spring rolls. Additional small sauce dishes can be placed around the dining table to spoon onto their stuffings if required. They should include at least one or more sauce dishes of hoisin sauce, ketchup laced with 2–3 teaspoons chilli sauce, and an equal mixture of sesame paste (or peanut butter), with soy sauce and 2 teaspoons of sesame oil; and soy sauce with 1 tablespoon English mustard and ½ tablespoon yellow bean sauce.

QUICK-FRIED DICED CHICKEN CUBES WITH WALNUTS IN SOY PASTE SAUCE

The dish is excellent for serving as a starter or appetizer. It is also excellent to eat with rice or fried rice.

Serves 4–5

8–10oz (225–275g) breast of chicken meat, cubed
2 tablespoons cornflour
1 egg white
1 teaspoon salt
4–5oz (100–150g) chopped walnuts
4 tablespoons vegetable oil

SAUCE:
2 slices ginger
1 tablespoon yellow bean sauce
½ tablespoon sugar
1½ tablespoons hoisin sauce
2 teaspoons cornflour blended in 2 tablespoons water
½ tablespoon soy sauce
¾ tablespoon lard

Dust the chicken with salt and cornflour and wet with the egg white. Prepare the ginger water by boiling ginger slices in 3 tablespoons water and reduce to 2 tablespoons, discarding the ginger. Heat the oil in a frying pan. Add the chicken and stir to separate the pieces for 1½ minutes. Add the walnuts and continue to stir-fry together for a further 1½ minutes. Remove with a slotted spoon and reserve.

Add the lard to the centre of the pan. When it has melted, add the yellow bean sauce, soy sauce, sugar, hoisin sauce and stir and mix them together with the ginger water. Mix and stir for ½ minute. Pour in the blended cornflour to stir and mix with the ingredients in the pan. Stir until the sauce thickens in the pan. Return the chicken and mix with the sauce in the pan. Stir and mix for 1–2 minutes. Finally, return the walnuts to the pan. Stir and mix them all together for a further ½ minute.

SLICED CHICKEN AND MUSHROOM SOUP WITH LETTUCE

After a succession of rich, savoury dishes this light soup will be a welcome change to the palate. Sip or drink it mouthful by mouthful during the meal.

Serves 4

1 4oz (100g) breast of chicken, sliced very thinly
1 tablespoon cornflour
1 egg white
1 teaspoon salt
6 medium-sized Chinese dried mushrooms
3 leaves cos lettuce, shredded
1¾ pints (1 litre) stock
1 chicken stock cube
2 slices root ginger, shredded
1 teaspoon sesame oil
pepper, to taste

Dust the chicken with salt and cornflour and wet with egg white. Parboil in boiling water for 1 minute, then drain and reserve. Soak the mushrooms in warm water for half an hour. Remove stem and cut each cap into quarters.

Heat the stock in a saucepan. Add root ginger, mushrooms and stock cube. Stir and leave to simmer for 6–7 minutes. Add the chicken, lettuce and continue to simmer for 3 minutes. Add salt and pepper to taste and sprinkle the top of the soup with sesame oil. Serve in a large soup-bowl or tureen for the guests to help themselves, or the soup can be divided into 4–5 small soup bowls (discarding the ginger at the bottom of the pan).

MEAT

RED-COOKED PORK (SOY-BRAISED LONG-COOKED PORK)
SZECHUAN HOT-FRIED CRISPY SHREDDED BEEF
RED-COOKED BRISKET OF BEEF (OR LEG OF BEEF)
MEAT-STUFFED STEAM BUNS (BAOTZE)
CLEAR-SIMMERED LAMB (OR MUTTON) WITH TURNIPS
CANTONESE CHAR SIU : BARBECUED ROAST PORK OR BEEF
WHITE-COOKED SLICED PORK
QUICK-FRIED BEEF IN OYSTER SAUCE
CHINESE WIND-DRIED SAUSAGES
CHINESE SAUSAGES STIR-FRIED WITH
FRENCH BEANS AND BEAN SPROUTS
CHINESE SAUSAGES IN RICE
QUICK-FRIED SPINACH

In Chinese cooking, meat can be cooked in a whole variety of ways. It can be cooked for a long time (several hours upwards) as in clear-simmering or soy-braising; or almost instantly, as in quick stir-fry cooking; or for a medium length of time, as in braising, sautéing or barbecue-roasting (Char Siu). Meat can be cooked whole, cut into shreds, sliced, diced or minced and made into cakes and meat-balls.

Because of these variations in length of cooking time and preparation, as well as the various different flavourings and extra ingredients that can be added, the number of meat dishes which are theoretically possible is almost alarming. However, as we do not have the space to explore all the highways and byways of Chinese meat cookery, we shall feature just a few of the principal cooking methods.

As with poultry, one of the most popular – almost classic – ways of cooking meat is to braise it with soy sauce, sugar and wine (often with minute additions of anise, or five-spice, and root ginger). What is most important in this kind of cooking is to maintain an even low temperature and cook for a good length of time. The fat and skin of the meat make an important contribution to the quality of these dishes, adding significantly to the flavour and richness of the gravy.

RED-COOKED PORK (SOY-BRAISED LONG-COOKED PORK)

Red cooking is unique to China. It is the use of soy sauce that gives the food a reddish colour and a rich flavour.

Serves 5–6

3–3½lb (1.3–1.5kg) belly of pork
5–6 tablespoons soy sauce (dark)
¾ pint (450ml) water (or stock)
1 tablespoon sugar
2 slices root ginger
3–4 pieces of star anise or ½ teaspoon five-spice powder (optional)
3–4 tablespoons dry sherry

Preheat the oven to 200°C (400°F, gas mark 6).

Cut the pork into oblong strips 2 by 1 inches (5 × 2.5cm). Add to a pan of briskly boiling water for 3–4 minutes, then drain. Place the pork in a medium-sized casserole. Add the soy sauce, water, sugar, ginger and star anise (or five-spice powder). Bring to the boil on top of the cooker, then put into the oven for 45 minutes. Skim off the excess fat and add the sherry. Reduce the heat to 180°C (350°F, gas mark 4) and cook for a further 45 minutes. Serve in the casserole, accompanied by rice and a vegetable dish.

SZECHUAN HOT-FRIED CRISPY SHREDDED BEEF

¾lb (350g) beef (topside)
4 eggs
¼lb (90g) cornflour
½ teaspoon salt
3 medium-sized carrots
oil for frying

SAUCE:
2 stalks spring onions
3 cloves garlic
2 chilli peppers
6 teaspoons sugar
3/4 tablespoons vinegar
1½ teaspoons soy sauce

Cut beef into thin slices, and then into matchstick shreds. Beat the eggs together with salt and cornflour. Add shredded beef to coat with batter.

Clean and cut carrots into similar matchstick shreds. Cut spring onions into 1½ inch sections (divide thicker stalks lengthwise into halves or quarters). Shred chillis, and chop garlic into coarse grains.

Deep-fry beef over a moderate heat for 5 minutes (or until crispy) and drain. Deep-fry carrots for 1½ minutes. Pour away the oil from the pan, leaving about 1½ tablespoons in the bottom. Add the spring onions, chilli and chopped garlic. Stir-fry them together for ¾ minute over a medium heat. Add the sugar, soy sauce and vinegar. Turn and mix them into a sauce. Return beef into the pan to stir-fry with the other ingredients over a high heat for about 10 seconds, and serve.

RED-COOKED BRISKET OF BEEF (OR LEG OF BEEF)

Serves 5–6

Repeat Red-Cooked Pork recipe, using brisket of beef instead of pork, but prolong the cooking by half an hour (giving 1 hour at high heat and 1 hour at the lower heat). Also increase the ginger used from 2 slices to 4–5 slices.

To provide variation to these red-cooked meat dishes, a quantity of chestnuts are often added to pork, and turnips added to beef, during the second stage of the cooking. Leg of beef can also be cooked in the same way, but the cooking will need to be prolonged by another 30–40 minutes (to about $1\frac{1}{4}$ hours at high heat, followed by a further $1\frac{1}{4}$ hours at the lower heat).

To complement these meat dishes a pure vegetable dish – such as 'quick-fried spinach' (see p. 41) – is often provided as a contrast in colour and texture.

MEAT-STUFFED STEAM BUNS (BAOTZE)

Meat and vegetable dishes are often eaten with steam buns (called baotze) which can be plain or stuffed with fillings. Like plain boiled rice these buns are used as bulk food to absorb the marvellous gravies and counterbalance the richness of the meat dishes.

DOUGH:
12–13oz (330–350g) flour
3 tablespoons sugar
$\frac{3}{4}$ tablespoon vegetable oil
1 teaspoon dried yeast
1 cup warm water

STUFFING:
8oz (225g) minced pork
2–3 spring onion stalks, cut into 1 inch
  (2.5cm) lengths
2–3 leaves Chinese cabbage, shredded
$\frac{1}{2}$ teaspoon salt
2–3 tablespoons vegetable oil
2 tablespoons lard
2 tablespoons soy sauce
1 tablespoon cornflour
2 tablespoons lard
1 tablespoon sesame oil

Place 3 cups of flour in a mixing bowl. Add half the sugar and the oil. Work together with your hands and blend well.

Put the yeast, remainder of flour and sugar and 4–5 tablespoons warm water in another bowl. Blend well together then add to the large mixing bowl. Work well together with your hands, adding the remaining water gradually. Knead the dough for 5–6 minutes. Cover with a damp cloth and leave in a warm place for 2 hours, or until it has doubled in size.

To make the stuffing, stir-fry the pork, onion, cabbage and salt in hot oil or fat in a small wok or frying-pan for 4–5 minutes. Add the soy sauce, oyster sauce and sesame oil and stir-fry for a further 2 minutes. Leave the stuffing to cool before using.

When it has risen, knead the dough again and shape into a long sausage, 2 inches (5cm) in diameter. Slice into 1 inch (2.5cm) thick rounds and form them into small dough-balls. Flatten each ball with your palms into a biscuit-shaped disc. Roll out each disc to form a thick pancake, thick in the middle and thin round the edges. Place a tablespoon of stuffing in the centre of each pancake and gather up the edges, closing them in a twist over the stuffing.

When the buns have been stuffed, place them well apart on a layer of cheesecloth on the rack of a steamer. Turn heat high under the steamer and steam vigorously for 15–17 minutes.

These steamed buns are often made and served without stuffings – then they are called man tous. They are made simply by steaming pieces of dough which have been pinched or broken off at 1 inch (2.5cm) intervals from the large sausage dough. These are steamed for 17–18 minutes and served to accompany savoury dishes. In Chinese tea-houses, where most of the stuffed steam buns are served, they are usually eaten as snacks.

CLEAR-SIMMERED LAMB (OR MUTTON) WITH TURNIPS

Traditionally, this dish is served by giving each guest a large bowl of noodles and spooning over some meat, soup and vegetables. The meat is eaten with a dip sauce, such as hoisin sauce, or soy sauce mixed with chilli sauce and tomato purée. This dish can also be eaten as a semi-soup dish in a meal where rice, rather than noodles, provides the bulk food.

Serves 6–8

3½–4lb (1.5–1.75kg) leg of lamb
3–4 slices root ginger
1 tablespoon salt
1¼lb (575g) turnips
2½ pints (1.4l) water
2 tablespoons light soy sauce
1 chicken stock cube
¼ pint (150ml) dry sherry
2–3 bundles watercress, roughly chopped

Preheat the oven to 180°C (350°F, gas mark 4).

Cut the lamb into 2 × 1 inch (5 × 2.5cm) bite-sized pieces. Place in boiling water for 3–4 minutes, then drain. Cut the turnips into triangular wedges.

Place the lamb pieces in a casserole. Add the ginger, salt, turnips and soy sauce and pour in the water. Bring to the boil on top of the cooker, then cover and put the casserole into the oven for 1¼ hours. Remove the lid and cook for a further hour at the same temperature. Add the watercress, adjust the seasoning, and cook for a further 5–6 minutes.

CANTONESE CHAR SIU: BARBECUED ROAST PORK OR BEEF

This dish looks very attractive. The marinade gives the meat a dark brown outside crust, while the inside is still juicy and only lightly cooked. The crunchiness of the lightly pickled cucumber makes a particularly good contrast of texture and flavour.

Serves 4–5

1½–1¾lb (675–800g) fillet of pork (or beef),
   cut into 2 × 2½ inch (5 × 6cm) strips

MARINADE:
1½ tablespoons yellow bean sauce
1 tablespoon dark soy sauce
1 tablespoon red bean-curd cheese
   (optional)
2 teaspoons sugar
1 tablespoon dry sherry
1 tablespoon vegetable oil

GARNISH:
1 medium-sized cucumber, thinly sliced
3 tablespoons sugar
4 tablespoons vinegar

Place the meat strips in a large bowl together with the marinade ingredients. Leave in a cool place for 1–2 hours, turning the meat over several times to let it absorb the flavours. Toss the cucumber slices in a bowl with the sugar and vinegar.

Pre-heat the oven to 220°C (425°F, gas mark 7). Remove the meat from the marinade and drain. Place the strips of meat on a wire rack, inside a roasting pan and place in the oven to roast (13–15 minutes for beef and 17–20 minutes for pork).

Place the meat, which should be very brown, and encrusted with the marinade, on a chopping board, and cut it across the grain into roughly circular discs of 1/6 inch (4mm) thickness. Lay slices on a serving dish, slightly overlapping. Surround the meat with sweet and sour cucumber slices laid out in similar fashion.

WHITE-COOKED SLICED PORK

Although the Chinese often cook highly seasoned meat, as, for example, red-cooked pork or red-cooked beef, they also cook meat by simply steaming or boiling. In these cases the meat is usually served with an array of dips.

There is a strong contrast in this recipe between the pale, mild-flavoured meat and the richly-flavoured coloured dips.

Serves 5–6

2½–3lb (1.25–1.5kg) belly of pork
4–5 slices root ginger
2–3 teaspoons salt

Place the pork in a small heavy saucepan. Add the ginger, salt and enough water to cover. Bring to the boil, skimming the surface to remove scum. Reduce heat to very low, and leave to simmer gently for 1¼ hours. Remove pork from pan, drain, and allow to cool. Cut down through skin, lean and fat into thin slices.

Arrange the pork slices on a serving dish in an overlapping fish-scale pattern and serve with the following dips.

DIP 1:
4 tablespoons dark soy sauce
2 tablespoons ketchup or tomato puree
1 tablespoon chilli sauce

DIP 2:
2 tablespoons light soy sauce
2 tablespoons wine vinegar
1 tablespoon chopped garlic

DIP 3:
2 tablespoons light soy sauce
1 tablespoon dark soy sauce
1½ tablespoons English mustard

DIP 4:
2 tablespoons light soy sauce
2 tablespoons shredded root ginger
1 tablespoon wine vinegar
1 tablespoon dry sherry

QUICK-FRIED BEEF IN OYSTER SAUCE

Serves 4–5

1lb (450g) beef steak (rump, tenderloin,
   fillet, flank), cut into 2 × 1½ inch (5 × 3.5cm)
   slices
1 tablespoon soy sauce
1½ teaspoons sugar
1 teaspoon salt
½ tablespoon cornflour
2 slices root ginger
4 tablespoons vegetable oil

SAUCE:
2 spring onion stalks, cut into shreds
2½ tablespoons oyster sauce
3 teaspoons light soy sauce
2 tablespoons good stock
1½ tablespoons dry sherry
2 teaspoons cornflour (blended in 2
   tablespoons water)

GARNISH:
12oz (350g) broccoli, divided into florets
5 tablespoons stock
1 teaspoon sesame oil

Place the beef in a mixing bowl. Add soy sauce, sugar, salt, cornflour, ginger and half a tablespoon oil. Mix well and leave to season for 10 minutes.

Heat remaining oil and sauce mixture in a wok or frying-pan. When hot, add the beef, and stir and turn it in the sauce for 2½ minutes over high heat. Remove and arrange it in the centre of a well-heated serving dish. Place the broccoli in the pan, add stock and sesame oil. Turn and stir the contents in the pan over high heat for 3–4 minutes. Remove with slotted spoon and arrange the broccoli around the beef at the centre of the serving dish. Serve with rice and other savoury dishes.

CHINESE WIND-DRIED SAUSAGES

One way of describing Chinese sausages is to say that they are like miniature salamis, about the size of average frankfurters and somewhat akin to salami in taste. They are normally steamed or briefly fried; or they can be stir-fried with vegetables. Being somewhat salty and spicy they are excellent to eat with plain boiled rice, cooked flaky and dry, or as rice porridge, which the Chinese eat at breakfast. The following recipes illustrate two popular ways in which it is used.

CHINESE SAUSAGES STIR-FRIED WITH FRENCH BEANS AND BEAN SPROUTS

Serves 5–6

3½ tablespoons vegetable oil
2 Chinese sausages, cut into thin strips
8oz (225g) French beans, shredded
½ chicken stock cube, dissolved in 3
    tablespoons hot stock
1 tablespoon soy sauce
8oz (225g) bean sprouts

Heat the oil in a wok or frying-pan. When hot add the sausage strips and stir-fry for half a minute. Remove from heat and continue to stir-fry away from heat for half a minute. Remove sausages with slotted spoon. Add the French beans to the pan. Stir-fry them in the oil in the pan for 2½ minutes. Add the stock and soy sauce. When it boils add the bean sprouts and mix and turn with all the other ingredients. Stir-fry them together for 2 minutes. Return the sausages to the pan and stir-fry them with the other ingredients for another minute.

CHINESE SAUSAGES IN RICE

Cut the sausages into 1 × 1½ inch (2.5 × 3.5cm) pieces. After the initial boiling of the rice, and the first 2–3 minutes simmering under cover, when the rice has absorbed a good proportion of the water in the pan, the sausage pieces can be stuck into the surface of the rice to steam and cook with the rice during the 4–5 minutes of simmering and 8–9 minutes of slow cooking in the remaining heat. When the rice is ready the sausages will be ready and they can be consumed together with other dishes.

QUICK-FRIED SPINACH

Serves 4–5

1½lb (675g) young spinach
5–6 tablespoons vegetable oil
2–3 cloves garlic, crushed
1½ teaspoons salt
2 teaspoons sugar
1½ tablespoons dry sherry
1 tablespoon soy sauce
1 tablespoon lard
1 teaspoon sesame oil

Wash and drain the spinach and cut off the stems.

Heat the oil in a wok or large saucepan. Add the garlic and spinach. Stir-fry for 1½ minutes over medium heat, turning and stirring all the time. Sprinkle with salt, sugar, sherry and soy sauce. Continue to cook for 1½ minutes, then add the lard and sesame oil, and turn and stir the spinach once more.

RABBIT STEW

This interesting recipe comes from the North and dates back to the 18th century.

Serves 2

8oz (250g) rabbit, chopped into bite sized
    pieces
$\frac{1}{4}$ pint (150ml) sherry
1 tablespoon soy sauce
$\frac{1}{2}$ teaspoon sesame oil
pinch cumin
2 spring onions
1 tablespoon barley

Cut the onion into 1 inch (3cm) lengths. Put the rabbit in a saucepan and cover with cold water. Bring slowly to the boil, then remove the rabbit and throw away the water. Rinse the rabbit and remove the scum. Put it with all the other ingredients in a casserole and simmer for $1\frac{1}{4}$ hours. Or cook in an oven at 180°C (350°F, gas mark 4) for $1\frac{1}{2}$ hours. If the gravy is not thick enough, remove the lid and boil for 5 minutes. Adjust the seasoning before serving.

FISH
AND
SEAFOOD

RED-COOKED FISH
SALT AND PEPPER FISH
STEAMED WHOLE FISH IN MUSHROOM AND
MEAT SAUCE
STIR-FRIED PRAWNS IN CRISPY NOODLE NEST
STIR-FRIED PRAWNS ON HOT CRACKLING RICE
PEKING SLICED FISH IN WHITE WINE SAUCE
PEKING FISH OMELETTE IN CHICKEN STOCK WITH
ONION, GARLIC AND GINGER SAUCE
CRAB-RICE WITH VEGETABLES
HOT AND SOUR SOUP WITH SHRIMPS AND
TOU FU BEAN CURD

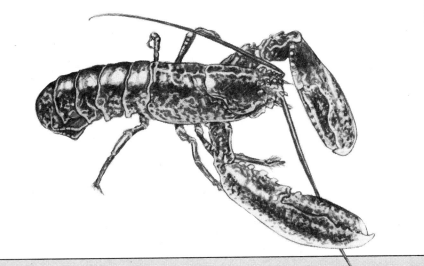

The number of ways in which fish and seafoods are cooked is more limited than meat. Extensive use is made of the strong-tasting ginger, onion and garlic. These are often further mixed with dried and salted foods, such as dried mushrooms, dried shrimps, bacon and various pickles. Through their strength of taste these ingredients seem to bring out the freshness in fish. Fish and seafoods are either cooked with very little additional sauce and seasonings, so that their light sweet freshness of taste is easily apparent, or they are given the reverse treatment by being smothered in strong-tasting foods and ingredients – such as fish in hot vinegar sauce, in hot soya paste sauce, in sweet and sour sauce, or soya-onion and ginger sauce.

The Chinese seem to make little distinction between the flavourings for meat and for fish, or seafood. Often they overlap, not only in the use of flavouring ingredients, but also in the basic materials used. For example, the Chinese seldom if ever make fish stock. When they need stock for fish they use chicken stock (they seem to blend admirably!). The same applies to sauces used with fish. They will not hesitate to use a meat-sauce, or sauce made with meat, with fish. They will use this in preference to sauces made from fish or seafoods. It seems that by using the qualities of different contrasting foods they are more able to achieve a balance of flavour. It is this inter-blending of flavours which makes Chinese cookery so intriguing. One of the basic Chinese fish dishes (as with meat and poultry) is Red-Cooked Fish or Fish Braised in Soy Sauce.

In China fish is probably eaten more often than meat. Fish, rice and vegetables seem to be the most common foods eaten by an average Chinese family. This is in spite of the fact that China is basically a large continent where meat should predominate. On the other hand, China has many thousands of miles of coastline, as well as countless rivers, tributaries, ponds and lakes, and the practice of fish-farming is widespread. It is quite common in China to see fresh fish on the table when you are many hundreds of miles inland.

RED-COOKED FISH

In spite of its simplicity, this is one of those dishes every Chinese remembers with nostalgia as one which 'Mother used to make'.

Serves 4–5

1½lb (675g) cod steaks or cutlets (or haddock, halibut etc)
2 teaspoons salt
2–3 tablespoons cornflour
4–5 slices root ginger, shredded
3–4 spring onion stalks, cut into 2 inch (5cm) pieces
6–7 tablespoons vegetable oil

SAUCE:
3 tablespoons soy sauce
3 teaspoons sugar
2 tablespoons stock
1 tablespoon dry sherry

Cut the fish into 4 or 5 equal-sized pieces. Rub them with salt and cornflour. Mix the ingredients in a mixing bowl.

Heat the oil in a frying-pan. When hot, add half the ginger and spring onion. Stir-fry for half a minute to flavour the oil, then push to one side. Add the fish piece by piece and fry for 2 minutes on either side.

Drain off excess oil, add the remaining onion and ginger and pour the mixed sauce over the fish. Baste the pieces of fish with the sauce and allow them to sauté for 2 minutes on either side.

To serve, transfer the fish to a heated serving dish, using the onion and ginger from the pan as dressing, and pour the remaining sauce in the pan over the fish. Some additional sauce may be created simply by adding 1½ tablespoons soy sauce, and 2 teaspoons cornflour blended in 2–3 tablespoons water and 1 tablespoon sherry into the pan and stirring them over high heat for 1–2 minutes. Pour the additional sauce over the fish.

SALT AND PEPPER FISH

Serves 4–5

1½lb (675g) filleted fish (cod, bass, bream, haddock, plaice etc)
½ pint (300ml) vegetable oil
2 teaspoons freshly ground black pepper
4 teaspoons salt
2 chilli peppers, deseeded and shredded
1 tablespoon vegetable oil

BATTER:
1 egg
4 tablespoons cornflour
4 tablespoons self-raising flour

Beat the ingredients for the batter in a mixing bowl until of a smooth consistency. Cut the fish into large bite-sized pieces. Add them to the bowl of batter and make sure they are evenly coated.

Heat the oil in a deep frying pan or deep-fryer. When hot – when a crumb will sizzle – add the fish pieces one by one. Turn them in the oil to fry evenly for 3 minutes. Remove with a slotted spoon and drain.

Meanwhile, heat 1 tablespoon oil in another wok or frying-pan. Add the salt, pepper and chillis. Stir-fry over medium heat for half a minute so that the seasonings are well spread over the pan. Add the fried pieces of fish to the pan in a single layer. Gently turn them over several times, so that each piece takes on the hot salty coating from the seasoned pan.

Transfer the fish to a heated serving dish. Because of its hot salty flavour, this is an excellent dish to serve with plain rice and lightly cooked vegetables.

STEAMED WHOLE FISH IN MUSHROOM AND MEAT SAUCE

This is similar in flavour to Red-Cooked Fish, but being a whole fish it is more suitable for formal occasions.

Serves 4–6

2lb (900g) fish (trout, mullet, bass, sole, salmon etc)
2 teaspoons salt
1½ tablespoons minced root ginger
1 tablespoon vegetable oil
1½ tablespoons dry sherry

MUSHROOM/MEAT SAUCE:
6 medium-sized Chinese dried mushrooms
3 tablespoons vegetable oil
4–5oz (100–150g) minced or shredded pork
1 tablespoon chopped Chinese pickle (winter pickle or snow pickle) (optional)
3/4 tablespoons yellow bean sauce
2 tablespoons soy sauce
1½ tablespoons hoisin sauce
2 slices root ginger, shredded
3 spring onion stalks, cut into matchsticks
3 tablespoons sugar
6 tablespoons stock
2 tablespoons dry sherry
1 tablespoon lard

Clean the fish and rub with salt, minced ginger, sherry and oil. Place the fish on a heat-proof dish, put it in a steamer or on a rack in a wok and steam vigorously for 15–18 minutes.

To prepare the sauce, soak the mushrooms in warm water for half an hour. Remove stems and cut caps into shreds. Heat the oil in a frying-pan and add the pork, mushrooms, pickle, bean sauce, soy sauce, hoisin sauce, ginger and half the spring onion, sugar and stock. Continue to stir and cook over medium heat for 3 minutes. Add lard and sherry. Stir and cook quickly to reduce the liquid in the pan to half.

Pour the hot sauce from the pan over the fish and sprinkle with the remaining spring onion.

STIR-FRIED PRAWNS IN CRISPY NOODLE NEST

Serves 4–5

2 tablespoons 'wood ear' fungi (optional)
½ pint (300ml) vegetable oil, for deep frying
8oz (225g) pea-starch transparent noodles
2 teaspoons cornflour
4 tablespoons chicken stock
3½ tablespoons oil
1½ teaspoons salt
1 tablespoon minced root ginger
1½ tablespoons spring onion shavings
12oz (350g) prawns (fresh or frozen)
4–6oz (100–175g) can of Chinese straw-
    mushrooms, or champignons
2–3 sticks green celery, cut into double
    matchstick strips
1½ teaspoons sugar
1 tablespoon light soy sauce
2 tablespoons white wine

Rinse and wash the 'wood ear' and soak in water for 10 minutes.

Heat the oil in a deep frying-pan or deep-fryer. When hot – when a crumb will sizzle when dropped into it – add the transparent noodles. They will immediately froth up into a large crinkly crispy mass. Lift them off and place on kitchen paper to drain. Blend the cornflour with the chicken stock.

Heat 3½ tablespoons oil in a frying-pan or wok. Add the salt, ginger, and half the spring onion. Stir them around a few times, add the prawns and stir-fry for 1 minute over high heat. Add the 'wood ears', mushrooms and celery. Stir-fry for 3 or 4 minutes. Add sugar and pour in the soy sauce, white wine, and chicken stock blended with cornflour. Heat until it boils, stirring, then sprinkle on the remaining spring onion shavings.

Arrange the crispy noodles in the form of a nest on a deep-sided serving dish and pour the contents of the pan over the centre of the nest. Serve as a starter to a party meal.

STIR-FRIED PRAWNS ON HOT CRACKLING RICE

Serves 4–5

When the sauce from the frying pan or wok is poured over the 'hot bed' in front of the guests at the table, it makes a sizzling, crackling noise. During the last war this dish was often styled 'Bombs Over the Enemy'!

Repeat the previous recipe, substituting crackling rice for crispy noodles. Crackling rice is made from the scrapings of rice which are normally stuck to the bottom of large rice pots, or pans in which rice is cooked in quantity. These are scraped off and further dried by putting them in an oven at low heat – 150°C (300°F, gas mark 2) – for 7–8 minutes, and left to dry further after the heat had been turned off. When required, these crispy rice scrapings are deep-fried in very hot oil for 2–2½ minutes, quickly drained, and transferred immediately to a hot serving dish, as a 'hot bed' for the remainder of the dish to be poured over it.

Although Peking and the North are not generally well known for their fish cookery as compared with the coastal provinces of the South-East, there are two fish dishes which are admirable and worthy of note:

PEKING SLICED FISH IN WHITE WINE SAUCE

The pure white of the fish and jet black of the 'wood ears' makes an attractive colour contrast.

Serves 4–6

1lb (450g) fillet of flat fish (plaice, sole, bream etc)
2 teaspoons salt
2 tablespoons cornflour
1 egg white
2–3 tablespoons black 'wood ear' fungi
3 teaspoons cornflour
3–4 tablespoons stock
½–1 pint (300–600ml) vegetable oil
2 slices root ginger
4–5 tablespoons white wine
2 teaspoons sugar
1 spring onion stalk, cut into shavings

Cut the fish into approximately 2 × 1½ inch (5 × 3.5cm) slices. Rub with salt and cornflour and wet thoroughly with egg white. Wash and soak the 'wood ears' in water for 10 minutes and drain. Mix the 3 teaspoons cornflour with stock until well blended.

Heat the oil in a deep frying-pan. When hot – when a crumb will sizzle when dropped into it – remove from the heat to cool for ¼ minute. Add the fish to the oil slice by slice and cook for 1 minute, turning them over once. Put the pan over medium heat for half a minute and remove again. Remove the fish carefully with a fish-slice, drain and keep warm.

Pour off all but 1 tablespoon of oil. Add the ginger and spring onion and fry for half a minute over medium heat. Remove ginger and add the 'wood ears'. Turn them over a few times. Add wine, sugar and blended cornflour. Stir quickly to mix well. When the sauce thickens and becomes translucent return the fish pieces to the pan. Stir gently into the sauce and cook for 1 minute. Sprinkle with the spring onion and serve.

PEKING FISH OMELETTE IN CHICKEN STOCK WITH ONION, GARLIC AND GINGER SAUCE

Serves 4–5

2 fish fillets, approximately 8oz (225g) each
1½ teaspoons salt
1½ teaspoons cornflour
5–6 eggs
6 tablespoons hot chicken stock
½ chicken stock cube
½ pint (300ml) vegetable oil
2 cloves garlic, thinly sliced
3 slices root ginger, shredded
2 spring onion stalks, shredded
1¼ tablespoons wine vinegar
1 tablespoon light soy sauce
2 tablespoons dry sherry
parsley and coriander (optional) for garnish

Rub the fish with salt and cornflour. Beat the eggs lightly in a mixing bowl. Add the fish to the mixing bowl and turn so that both pieces are well coated. Dissolve the stock cube in the stock.

Heat the oil in a large frying-pan or wok. When hot – when a crumb will sizzle when dropped into it – add the fish, placing the two pieces carefully one beside the other. Pour the remainder of the beaten egg on top. Shake the pan so that the egg and fish do not stick to the bottom. When the egg is set, pour away all the oil, reduce heat to low and sprinkle the garlic, ginger and spring onion around the edges of the omelette. Turn the omelette over with a fish slice. Pour on vinegar, soy sauce, chicken stock and sherry. Place a lid over the pan and leave to simmer gently for 2–3 minutes. Using a fish slice, transfer the fish omelette to a serving dish. Pour the remaining sauce on top and garnish with sprigs of coriander and parsley.

CRAB-RICE WITH VEGETABLES

In China crab-rice is a dish which occurs frequently only along the South-East coastline, where it is cooked simply by burying large chopped-up pieces of crab (including the shell) in half-cooked or uncooked rice and leaving them to cook by steaming them together. When the rice is served it is impregnated with the flavour of the crab, and the vegetable with which it is cooked. Since Westerners are less adept at dealing with bones and shells than the Chinese, this dish has been adapted.

Serves 5–6

1lb (450g) rice
3 tablespoons vegetable oil
2 teaspoons salt
8oz (225g) leeks, cut into ½ inch (1cm) pieces
1 tablespoon lard
2 cloves garlic, thinly sliced
8oz (225g) crab-meat
¼ pint (150ml) chicken stock (with ½ chicken stock cube dissolved in it)
2–3 shrimps (fresh or frozen)
4oz (100g) peas

Wash rice, place in a saucepan and cover with its own volume of water. Bring to the boil and simmer over minimum heat for 2 minutes. Turn off the heat, cover and leave rice to steam in the remaining heat for 5 minutes. By this time the rice will be semi-cooked and almost dry. Pour the rice into a large heat-proof bowl or dish and make a hollow in the middle.

Heat the oil in a frying-pan. Add the salt and leeks and stir-fry for 2½ minutes. Then use them to line the hollow made in the rice. Add the lard and garlic to the pan and stir over medium heat for half a minute. Add the crab-meat and stir-fry with the garlic for 1 minute. Spoon into the hollow in the rice, on top of the leeks. Pour the chicken stock into the pan and add the shrimps and peas. Bring to the boil quickly, then pour them evenly around the edges of the leeks, allowing the sauce to seep down into the rice.

Cover the top of the bowl with aluminium foil and place in a steamer. Steam vigorously for 10–12 minutes.

HOT AND SOUR SOUP WITH SHRIMPS AND TOU FU BEAN CURD

As the dishes in this chapter are comparatively light, we shall serve a soup which is slightly heavier and strong-tasting. Almost any ingredients can be added to the soup so long as it helps to strengthen its flavour.

Serves 4–5

6–8 medium-sized Chinese dried
  mushrooms
1–2 tablespoons dried shrimps
2½ pints (1.4 l) stock
1–2 chicken stock cubes
2 slices root ginger, shredded
2 medium-sized onions, thinly sliced
2–3oz (50–75g) chicken meat (cooked or
  uncooked)
2–3oz (50–75g) filleted fish, shredded
1–2 cakes *tou fu* bean curd, cut into small
  lumps
2 teaspoons salt
2–3 shrimps (fresh or frozen)
1½ tablespoons chopped spring onion
2 eggs

HOT AND SOUR SAUCE:
¼ pint (150ml) stock
2 tablespoons soy sauce
4–5 tablespoons wine vinegar
½ teaspoon freshly ground pepper
2 tablespoons cornflour

Soak dried mushrooms and dried shrimps in water for 15 minutes and drain, reserving the water. Discard mushroom stems and cut caps into shreds. Stir the sauce ingredients together until well blended.

Heat the stock in a large saucepan with the stock cubes. When hot add the dried shrimps, mushrooms, ginger and onion. Simmer for 15 minutes, then add the chicken, fish, bean curd, salt and shrimps. When the mixture starts to boil, reduce heat and simmer for 5 minutes. Sprinkle with the spring onion and stir in the sauce slowly so as to blend with the other ingredients. Beat the eggs lightly and steam slowly into the soup along the prongs of a fork, trailing it over the surface of the soup. When the eggs set, the soup is ready.

PLAICE IN SOY SAUCE

Serves 2

8oz (250g) plaice or dab
1 leek

SAUCE:
3 tablespoons sherry
3 tablespoons soy sauce
1 teaspoon sugar
3 tablespoons water

Wash and clean the fish, leaving on the head and tail. Wash and cut the leek into 1-inch (3cm) pieces. Put the seasoning sauce in a saucepan and bring to the boil. Add the fish and leek, cover and simmer for 20 minutes over a very low heat. Adjust the seasoning and serve.

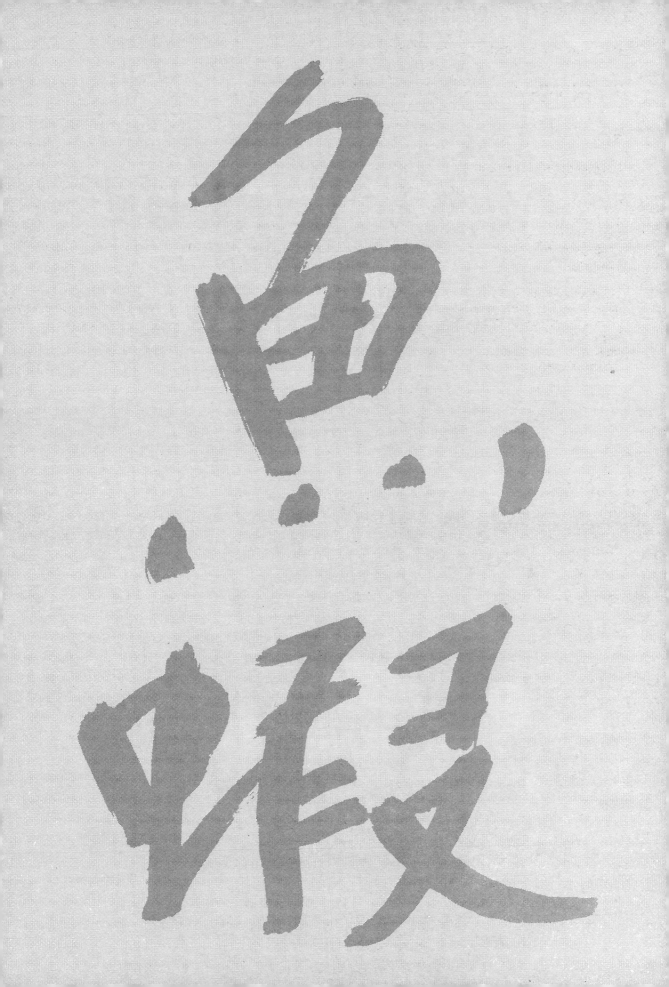

菜

VEGETARIAN AND VEGETABLE DISHES

COLD-TOSSED BEAN CURD
SHANGHAI COLD-TOSSED NOODLES
VEGETABLE FRIED RICE
SPINACH AND RADISH SALAD
SPINACH AND MUSHROOM SOUP
CRISPY SEAWEED
FU-YUNG CAULIFLOWER
RED-COOKED CABBAGE
QUICK-FRIED MIXED SHREDDED VEGETABLES
MIXED VEGETABLES IN CHICKEN FAT SAUCE
BRAISED AUBERGINE WITH COURGETTES

The Chinese eat far more vegetables than meat. The average family probably does not eat meat more than a couple of times a month. Most of the time, meat is used more for flavouring than for consuming in bulk. As a result, the Chinese have become experts in making savoury vegetables. By the same token they have also become experts in making vegetables smooth and succulent by introducing different types of oil or fat into the cooking at different stages. It is in the combination of these qualities of savouriness and succulence with the natural flavour and sweetness of fresh vegetables that Chinese cooking excels.

In the past, in many other parts of the world, vegetables have often been regarded as the food of the poor. Since few of the poor have ever had the time, opportunity or resources to develop culinary arts, much of Western vegetable cookery has until recently been in a fairly unsophisticated state.

It is only in very recent times, probably because of the heightening concern over health and health foods, that there has been a sudden surge of interest in vegetables and consequently in vegetable cookery. But in charting this new area of interest and awareness there does not seem to be much past literature to provide guidelines. This is where the Chinese experience in vegetable cookery can make a contribution.

The Chinese tradition of presenting a whole array of dishes at a meal, in varying shapes and sizes of dishes or bowls with a profusion of colour, taste, texture and aroma, creates a positive 'garden' on the dining table which must appeal to the British botanic and gardening instincts. If these interests and instincts could be combined with the Chinese experience and tradition it might even be possible one day to initiate a culinary event centred around vegetable cookery which would arouse as much interest as the Chelsea Flower Show.

COLD-TOSSED BEAN CURD

For a special occasion this can be heaped inside a scraped-out melon or marrow, then chilled. It makes an excellent starter.

Serves 4–6

2 tablespoons dried shrimps
3 tablespoons wine vinegar
2 teaspoons caster sugar
2 tablespoons soy sauce
1½ tablespoons vegetable oil
½ chicken stock cube
3 tablespoons stock
1½ tablespoons sesame paste
2 teaspoons sesame oil
2–2½ cakes of *tou fu* bean curd, cut into lumps
1½ tablespoons finely chopped *Szechuan Ja Chai* pickle
1½ tablespoons finely chopped *Tienjin Tung Chai* or winter pickle (optional)
1½ tablespoons Red Oil (chilli oil) or chilli sauce
2 tablespoons finely chopped spring onion
1 tablespoon finely chopped crushed garlic

Soak the dried shrimps in a cupful of water for 20 minutes. Drain and chop finely. Place in a small bowl with the wine vinegar to soak for half an hour. In another bowl, add the sugar to the soy sauce and vegetable oil and mix well together. Dissolve the stock cube in the stock, add sesame paste and sesame oil and mix well together.
Place the *tou fou* bean curd in a large bowl. Sprinkle evenly with the two pickles (the *Tienjin* winter pickle and the *Szechuan Ja Chai* – if available). Sprinkle in succession with the dried shrimps and vinegar, soy sauce, sugar and oil, stock with sesame paste and sesame oil, chopped spring onion and garlic.

Place the bowl in the refrigerator for half an hour just before serving. The coolness of the chilled *tou fou* makes a good contrast to the hot savoury dishes following.

SHANGHAI COLD-TOSSED NOODLES

Serves 4

The flavourings used here are exactly the same as in the previous recipe, except that the quantity of vinegar, stock and soy sauce should all be increased by half a tablespoon each and the main food used will be boiled noodles or spaghetti. If noodles are used, they should be the large fat variety, and should be boiled 6–7 minutes and drained; and if spaghetti is used it will need to be boiled for 15–17 minutes and drained.

In the cold tossed noodles, which is normally a summer dish in Shanghai, shredded celery (shredded to matchstick-size strips) or shredded lettuce or bean sprouts can all be tossed and mixed into the noodles. Although this dish can be reasonably substantial, it is a good item to serve as an appetizer.

VEGETABLE FRIED RICE

A well-composed fried rice dish should have at least two separate classes of ingredients: the salty and savoury, and the fresh-tasting. Combining these two distinct qualities with the blandness of the rice, the end product is much more appealing than if the ingredients had been thrown together haphazardly. Because of the large proportion of fresh vegetables, this dish tastes exceptionally sweet and fresh.

Serves 4–5

2 hard-boiled eggs
1 tablespoon chopped dried shrimps
2½ tablespoons vegetable oil
1 medium-sized onion, thinly sliced
1½ tablespoons finely chopped Chinese salted pickle, winter pickle or snow pickle
1 small can Chinese straw mushrooms or champignons
2–3oz (50–75g) soy-braised bamboo shoots (canned), finely chopped
1¼lb (575g) cooked rice
3 tablespoons stock
1½ tablespoons light soy sauce

FRESH VEGETABLES:
3oz (75g) fresh firm mushrooms, diced
1 red sweet pepper, diced
1 small cucumber, diced
3oz (75g) bean sprouts
2oz (50g) peas
2 small tomatoes, chopped
2oz (50g) sweet corn
2 spring onion stalks, shredded
3 tablespoons vegetable oil

Cook the hard-boiled eggs in soy sauce for 5 minutes and leave to stand in the sauce for another 5 minutes, then dice. Soak the dried shrimps in water for 30 minutes, then drain and chop finely. Heat the oil in a saucepan. Add the sliced onion and stir-fry over high heat for ½ minute. Add dried shrimps, pickles and bamboo-shoots. Stir-fry for a quarter minute then reduce heat to low. Add the rice and chopped soy-eggs. Stir the ingredients together for 2 minutes until evenly mixed then remove from heat.

Heat 3 tablespoons oil in a separate pan. When hot, add all the fresh vegetables. Stir-fry lightly over medium heat for 3 minutes. Add stock. Turn and stir-fry them around once more. Empty the contents of the second pan into the pan containing the rice. Turn and stir all the ingredients together until they are evenly mixed. Sprinkle 1½ tablespoons light soy sauce over the fried rice and serve.

SPINACH AND RADISH SALAD

This makes an excellent starter to any meal.

Serves 5–6

1½–2lb (657–900g) spinach
12oz (350g) bright red radishes
¼ chicken stock cube
2 tablespoons stock
2 tablespoons salt
2 tablespoons olive oil
¾ tablespoon sesame oil
1½ tablespoons light soy sauce
2 teaspoons caster sugar
large pinch freshly ground pepper

Place the spinach in a large saucepan, pour on a large kettleful of boiling water and leave to soak for 1½ minutes. Drain and press between sheets of kitchen paper. Chop the drained spinach into ½ inch (1cm) slices and place in a large china salad bowl. Dissolve the stock cube in the stock.

Give each radish a heavy blow with the side of a chopper after trimming. Sprinkle heavily with salt and leave for half an hour. Rinse quickly under running water and drain.

Sprinkle the oils evenly over the spinach in the bowl, followed by the stock, soy sauce, sugar and pepper. Toss well, then arrange the radishes on top of the spinach. The contrast between the bright red of the radish and the dark green of the spinach makes for an attractive presentation, whilst the rich savoury freshness of the spinach contrasts well in the palate with the sharp unexpected saltiness of the radish.

SPINACH AND MUSHROOM SOUP

With three cold dishes and a fried rice – the latter is a dry dish – a soup is called for. The spinach and mushroom soup, like most Chinese soups, is easy to make and should fill the bill.

Serves 4–5

6–8 medium Chinese dried mushrooms (or 5oz (150g) fresh button mushrooms)
12oz (350g) spinach
2 pints (1.15 l) stock
1 chicken stock cube
salt and pepper, to taste
1½ tablespoons light soy sauce
1½ teaspoons sesame oil

Soak the dried mushrooms in water for half an hour. Discard stems and cut each cap into quarters.

Heat the stock in a large saucepan. Add the mushrooms and stock cube and bring to the boil. Reduce heat to low and simmer gently for 8 minutes. Adjust for seasoning with salt and pepper. Add the spinach and allow to simmer for a further 3 minutes. Sprinkle the soup with soy sauce and sesame oil. Serve in a large soup tureen or divide into individual bowls.

CRISPY SEAWEED

2lb (900g) selected spring greens (cabbage)
2oz (50g) almonds, split
oil for deep frying
1½ teaspoons caster sugar
½ teaspoon salt
¼ teaspoon monosodium glutamate

Roll cabbage leaves into a firm roll. Cut, shave cabbage with a razor-sharp knife into the thinnest possible shavings. Wash and dry thoroughly in a breezy spot either by spreading them out on kitchen paper or in a large wire colander (for about 1 hour). Deep fry or shallow fry the almonds until crispy.

Heat the oil in a large pan until it is about to smoke, and remove from the heat for ¼ minute. Add all the spring green shavings. Stir and return pan to heat and fry for 2½ minutes. Remove and put aside for 1 minute. Return the greens to fry for a second time for ½ minute. Remove, drain and place on kitchen paper to eliminate as much grease as possible.

Serve on a well heated serving dish and sprinkle evenly with sugar, salt and monosodium-glutamate (MSG).

MSG must be used sparingly. When used in quantities of less than ½ teaspoon, as with salt and pepper, it can have no ill effects. When abused and used in quantities, it may produce what is known as 'The Chinese Syndrome', but it will not have effects any more devastating than if salt or pepper were used in similar quantities. Therefore in cooking treat MSG as if it were salt or pepper.

FU-YUNG CAULIFLOWER

A good dish to accompany rice especially when the majority of other dishes on the table are gravy-brown in colour, due to the predominance of soy sauce.

Serves 5–6

1 large cauliflower, about 2½lb (1.25kg)
3–4oz (75–100g) breast of chicken, minced
4–5 tablespoons chicken stock
1 teaspoon each salt and pepper (to taste)
1 tablespoon cornflour
5–6 tablespoons milk
2½ tablespoons vegetable oil
2oz (50g) ham, finely chopped

Divide the cauliflower into florets. Parboil them in boiling water for 5 minutes and drain. Blend cornflour in 4 tablespoons water.

Mix the minced chicken with stock, milk, blended cornflour, salt and pepper to taste, until well blended.

Heat the oil in a deep frying-pan. Pour in the minced chicken mixture. Stir continuously until it thickens into a white sauce. Add the cauliflower florets and turn in the sauce until every piece is well covered. Reduce heat to low and cook the cauliflower gently in the sauce for 2 to 3 minutes.

Turn the cauliflower out on a large serving dish and pour the white sauce on top. Sprinkle cauliflower and sauce with chopped ham and serve.

RED-COOKED CABBAGE

This is one of the simplest and yet one of the most effective cabbage dishes.

Serves 4–6

1 medium savoy cabbage (or Chinese celery cabbage), sliced
2 slices root ginger
3 tablespoons vegetable oil
2 tablespoons butter
2 teaspoons sugar
1 chicken stock cube
4–5 tablespoons hot water
3 tablespoons soy sauce

Crumble stock cube and dissolve in the hot water.

Heat the oil in a saucepan. Add the ginger, stir in the oil for half a minute and remove. Add the cabbage, stock, soy sauce, sugar and butter. Bring to the boil, stirring. Reduce heat to low and allow to cook gently, with a lid for 12–15 minutes. By this time the vegetable should have become very tender and savoury. Turn it in the sauce a few times.

Serve the cabbage in large serving bowl.

QUICK-FRIED MIXED SHREDDED VEGETABLES

Serves 4–5

4 tablespoons vegetable oil
2 dried red chilli peppers, deseeded and shredded
2 green chilli peppers, deseeded and shredded
3 slices root ginger, shredded
1 medium cucumber, cut into shreds
3–4oz (75–100g) bamboo shoots
1 red pepper, deseeded and shredded
2 celery sticks, shredded
2 spring onion stalks, shredded
2 teaspoons salt
1½ tablespoons oyster sauce
1½ tablespoons light soy sauce
4 tablespoons chicken stock
2 teaspoons sugar
3–4oz (75–100g) ham, cut into matchstick strips
3 teaspoons sesame oil

Heat the oil in a large frying-pan. When hot, add the chilli peppers and ginger. Stir-fry for 1 minute and then add all the other vegetables. Stir them over high heat for 3 minutes. Add oyster sauce, soy sauce, stock, salt, sugar and ham. Turn and toss them together evenly. Sprinkle with sesame oil and serve.

MIXED VEGETABLES IN CHICKEN FAT SAUCE

Serves 6

12oz (350g) **Chinese cabbage**
4–5oz (100–150g) **can button mushrooms**
8oz (225g) **can miniature corns**
4oz (100g) **snow peas, or mange-touts**
1 **small red pepper, cut into strips**
3 **tablespoons vegetable oil**
2 **teaspoons salt**
6 **tablespoons chicken stock**
½ **chicken stock cube**
3 **teaspoons cornflour, blended in 2 tablespoons water**
4 **tablespoons chicken fat**

Cut each large cabbage leaf into quarters and the small leaves into halves. Dissolve the stock cube in the stock and blend with the cornflour. Drain the canned vegetables.

Heat the oil in a deep frying-pan. Add the cabbage, snow peas and peppers. Stir-fry for 2 minutes. Add the mushrooms and miniature corns. Sprinkle with salt and add 3 tablespoons water. Bring back to the boil, reduce heat and simmer gently for 3 minutes. Pour the blended chicken stock and cornflour mixture into the pan and turn the vegetables over in the thickening sauce. Cook gently together for 1 minute.

Pour the vegetables and sauce into a deep-sided serving dish. Heat the chicken fat. When very hot pour over the vegetables and serve.

BRAISED AUBERGINE WITH COURGETTES

Excellent with rice and as a contrast to milder-tasting dishes.

Serves 5–6

3–4 **medium courgettes**
2 **medium aubergines**
2 **tablespoons dried shrimps**
4 **large Chinese dried mushrooms**
2oz (50g) **hot** *Szechuan Ja Chai* **pickle**
2 **cloves garlic**
4 **tablespoons vegetable oil**
3oz (75g) **minced pork**
1½ **teaspoons salt**
2 **tablespoons Szechuan soy-garlic-chilli paste** *(tou-ban-jiang)*
8–10 **tablespoons chicken stock**
2 **tablespoons lard**
2 **tablespoons soy sauce**
2 **tablespoons hoisin sauce**
2 **tablespoons oyster sauce**
2 **sprays coriander leaves**

Clean and cut the courgettes and aubergines into thick discs and then further cut the latter into halves. Soak shrimps and mushrooms in water for half an hour. Remove and discard mushroom stems. Roughly chop the mushroom caps, pickle, garlic and shrimps.

Heat the oil in a deep frying-pan or saucepan. When hot, add the minced meat and all the chopped ingredients. Stir them over high heat for 2 minutes. Add salt, soy-garlic-chilli paste and chicken stock. Stir together into a sauce. Add the aubergine and courgettes to the sauce, stir several times, reduce heat and leave to cook gently in the sauce for 6–7 minutes (or until nearly all the stock has evaporated). Stir 3–4 times in the process.

Add the lard to the pan, together with the soy sauce, hoisin sauce and oyster sauce. When it comes to the boil, stir a few times. Sprinkle with coriander leaves and serve in a heated deep-sided dish.

GLOSSARY

Aniseed: a powder from the seeds of anise, tasting rather like fennel.

Star anise: a dried, brown star-shaped spice used in flavouring Chinese stews.

Barbecue sauce: a yellow-bean paste. A piquant, sweet sauce used as a seasoning in meat dishes.

Bamboo shoots: soft flesh from young bamboo shoots, with a texture rather like new potato. Sold in cans. Can be kept after opening by boiling every 3–4 days in the juice and returning to a clean container.

Bean curd: made from soya beans and very rich in protein. Used in a wide range of Chinese dishes, particularly vegetable dishes. Sold fresh in 3 inch (8cm) squares. Also sold dried in packets.

Bean sprouts or bean shoots: sold fresh or canned, they can also be grown from seeds available from garden centres. Follow the instructions on the packet.

Black beans: fermented and salted. These are processed black beans with a characteristic flavour, used in both fish and meat dishes. They keep for many months in a refrigerator.

Chilli bean paste: a very hot seasoning sauce, used particularly in Szechuan cooking and, judiciously, as a table dip. Must not be overheated.

Chilli oil: a hot-flavoured oil, sold in bottles. Can be made by frying fresh or dried chillis in a little cooking oil for about five minutes, then straining the oil.

Chilli sauce: a hot sauce used for dipping.

Ginger: the fresh root of the ginger plant (powdered ginger is most definitely not satisfactory) is the principal flavour in Chinese food. Store in a dry, airy place.

Hoisin sauce: a sauce similar to Chinese brands of barbecue sauce but made with vinegar, so it is more of a sweet-sour sauce. The best variety comes from the mainland of China. Barbecue sauce can be substituted.

Monosodium glutamate: a powder used widely in Western pre-prepared foods to enhance the flavour. Sold either in cans ('Vetsin') or packets labelled 'MSG'.

Mushrooms: dried, their flavour is unique and they form an important part of many Chinese dishes. Soak in warm water for 20 minutes before cooking. Sold in polythene bags by weight, they keep for a long time. Ordinary, fresh mushrooms are a poor substitute.

Oil: the Chinese favour peanut oil for cooking. It has a distinctive flavour but ordinary Western cooking oil can be used instead. The smoking temperature of peanut oil is 300°F/150°C, while that of Western cooking oil is 450°F/232°C. The Chinese also use lard and chicken dripping which is easily obtained by rendering down any lumps of fat which come with the pork or chicken.

Oyster sauce: a Cantonese sauce, slightly fishy and very appetizing. Often served over vegetables.

Pickled cabbage or mustard-green: salted cabbage sold in cans. Used in stews, soups and stir-fries. To keep, remove from the can and store in a refrigerator. Rinse before use.

Pepper: many Chinese cooks use only Szechuan pepper, an aromatic type, or chillis.

Pickled cucumbers: in either soy or brine. Sold in jars or cans. Used in soups, or eaten as they are with rice porridge for breakfast or as a cold dish.

Sesame oil: one of the most important flavours in Chinese cooking. Sold in bottles.

Sesame paste: a nutty-flavoured, oil paste, rather like peanut butter. A more bland version, known as tahina, can be bought from Greek or Indian grocers. A substitute can be made by mixing a little sesame oil with peanut butter.

Sesame seeds: black or white sesame seeds are used in both meat and sweet dishes.

Soy sauce: the basic sauce of all Chinese cooking. It is made from soya beans by a process of hydrolysis and gives a savoury taste. There are various grades of soy. Recommended varieties are Soy Superior and Mushroom Soy, both from the Pearl River Bridge in mainland China. A light soy sauce makes an excellent table sauce.

Szechuan preserved vegetable: a form of hot, pickled cabbage stalk sold in cans. Rinse before use. Keeps well in a refrigerator.

Tientsin preserved vegetables: a slightly sweetish dry pickled cabbage used in duck soup and with rice porridge. Sold in round stone jars.

SUPPLIERS

Ken Lo's Kitchen
14 Eccleston Street
London SW1

Cheong Leen Supermarket
4–10 Tower Street
Cambridgeshire Close
London WC2

Loon Fung Provisions
42/43 Gerrard Street
London W1

Chung Nam Provisions
162 Bromsgrove Street
Birmingham 5

Chung Wah Trading Centre
31/32 Great Georges Square
Liverpool 1

Chung Ying Supermarket
63 Cambridge Street
Glasgow

Friendship Stores
29 Lady Lane
Leeds 2

Hung Keng and Co
169 London Road
Sheffield 2

Wing Hing Loon Supermarkets
46 Faulkner Street
Manchester M1 4FH

Yau's Chinese Foodstore
9 St Mary's Street
Southampton

INDEX